Contents

Features

Children's Paris	26
Soup for the soul	33
Going for a song	55
Food, glorious food	75
Paris on the screen	88
French bread	110

Maps

Versailles	99
Centre	130
Louvre-Opéra	132
Montmartre	133
Paris	fold-out
Métro	fold-out

Symbols:
- ★   Our favourites
- Ⓜ   Métro station
- ⓇⒺⓇ   RER station
- ♿   Wheelchair access

cityLights	5
cityPast	9
citySights	19
The Islands and the Seine	20
Latin Quarter	28
Saint-Germain, Montparnasse	36
Invalides and Eiffel Tower	46
Louvre and Palais Royal	50
Halles, Marais	58
Bastille, Bercy, Belleville	66
Grands Boulevards	72
Champs-Elysées and the West	78
Montmartre and the North	90
Around Paris	96
cityBites	101
cityNights	113
cityFacts	119
Index	134

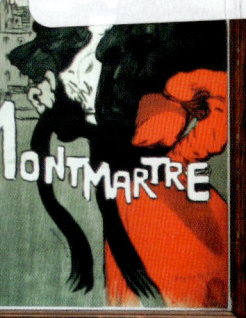

cityLights

You'll Be Back

There must be something infectious in the air of Paris, making you want to go back time and again. The addiction strikes as soon as you arrive. Certainly the first visit is no more than an appetizer, as unassuming as a slice of pâté and a pickle on the kind of bread that no one could ever imitate at home. You may have seen the new Louvre—well, the *Mona Lisa* and an hour of trudging—and looked down on the city from the Eiffel Tower and gazed up at it from a pleasure boat on the Seine, but there's still so much more to do! You've hardly spoken to a genuine Parisian, or figured out exactly what makes them so utterly *chic*. You've barely attempted the bright, efficient transit system and there hasn't been much time or energy to walk along the river banks or under the giant chestnut trees, in what must be the world's most walkable capital. You can't quite remember whether you are on the Right Bank or the Left, or what the difference means. The itch has begun; a return trip to Paris is definitely due. Almost before you've got to grips with the first one.

Up the Cathedral

If you're not on the Right Bank or the Left, chances are you're on the streamlined island in the middle of the Seine, the Ile de la Cité. And the wonderful medieval cathedral you're looking at is Notre-Dame de Paris. You could spend an hour in the *parvis* out front just marvelling at the harmony and the sculptural details. The view from the back is just as spectacular. But go inside, too, and climb up the stairs in the tower for one of the city's greatest panoramas.

Heaven only knows, Paris has enough superb churches to keep a pilgrim busy round the clock. But nearby you'll always find a café to catch your breath, a leafy park to rest and watch the people passing by, or a restaurant to revive your faith in the creativity of France's winemakers and cooks.

The New Paris

Even if you've seen all the monuments, you'd still have to return to catch up with the breathtaking changes in the city. The past few years have added revolutionary buildings,

starting with I.M. Pei's glass pyramid in the main courtyard of the enlarged, vastly improved Louvre. From here, look across the Tuileries to other echoes of Egypt in Place de la Concorde—the obelisk, now topped by a shining golden pyramidion. Another kind of magic turned an abandoned railway station into the Musée d'Orsay,

CITYLIGHTS

transforming it into the perfect setting for the Impressionist collections.

Spectacular in a bigger way is the Arche de la Défense, a hollow marble cube opening new perspectives of architecture and city planning. Then there is the ambitious City of Music, the City of Science and Industry enlightening the site of the former abattoirs; and the final monument to the era of François Mitterrand, the (Very) Great Library. No one has ever skimped on culture in the City of Light.

It's Always Sunny

Somehow the imagination paints a Paris as sunny as a summer picnic. In truth, the city sometimes sees more rainfall than London. So say the statistics—but what does the weatherman know about romance? Wait out a sudden shower in a noisy bistro, a department store crammed with flair or a musty bookshop. Afterwards, even the puddles reflect the city's grace: the wrought-iron railings, the shop-fronts, the sculpture. Water is an essential part of Paris, from the fountains and the ponds for mini-sailboats to the irresistible call of the river.

BEAT THE QUEUES

Admission to the national museums is free on the first Sunday of the month (daily for EU nationals under 26), and the permanent collections of municipal museums are free all the time. Otherwise, ticket prices vary. If you intend to do a lot of museum-visiting, consider buying a PARIS MUSEUM PASS, obtainable at the Paris Tourist Office, at FNAC outlets, on www.parismuseumpass.com and from the museums and monuments themselves. Three versions are available, valid for 2, 4 or 6 days for 32, 48 or 64 euros.

cityPast

Gauls and Romans
Paris was founded at the spot where the trade route from the Rhine district intersected with the Seine at its most easily fordable point—the Ile de la Cité, now the very centre of France's capital city. Around the 3rd century BC, this island was called Lutetia (Lutèce), inhabited by the Parisii, a tribe of Celtic fishermen. The original settlement didn't amount to much.
The right bank of the river was too marshy for building, so Paris expanded on the left bank, on the land that is now, by almost total coincidence, called the Latin Quarter.

The fortified city fell to one of Julius Caesar's lieutenants in 52 BC. Under the pax Romana of the 1st century, Lutetia became a Roman town, spreading over the Montagne Sainte-Geneviève on the left bank. During this period of prosperity, great villas, arenas and baths were built and a brilliant Gallo-Roman culture developed.

Frankish Capital

By the end of the 5th century, the Franks had become the masters of Paris. They were converted to Christianity by their leader Clovis, who made the city the capital of a Christian Frankish Kingdom. Under Clovis and his Merovingian successors, the city spilled over onto the banks of the Seine as churches and chapels were built, including the abbey of Saint-Germain-des-Prés. Charlemagne, the second Carolingian king, founded a vast empire stretching from Ebre to the Elbe. He chose Aix-la-Chapelle as its capital, and Paris became something of a backwater.

During the reign of Charles the Bald, first King of France, the Vikings landed on the Normandy beaches, advanced up the Valley of the Seine and besieged Paris in 885.

Medieval Paris

In 987, the nobles and clergy elected Hugues Capet, Count of Paris, the King of France. With Paris as his capital, he founded a dynasty that endured for centuries. His successors expanded the city and its power, and by the 12th century Paris had taken on its present social pattern: political authority on the island, culture on the Left Bank, business on the Right.

Under Philippe Auguste in the 12th and 13th centuries, the streets were partially paved, the cathedral of Notre-Dame was completed and a rampart was constructed, defended by the Louvre fortress. The right bank, around the market of Les Halles, became the centre of commercial activity under the control of the river traders' guild, holding the monopoly of navigation on the Seine. In 1215, Pope Innocent III granted a charter to the University of Paris. The colleges were established on the left bank, among them one founded by Robert de Sorbon in 1257—la Sorbonne. The students were taught in Latin, hence the name that stuck: the Latin Quarter. By the end of the 13th century, Paris had become the largest city in Christian Europe with 80,000 inhabitants.

At the beginning of the 14th century, rivalry between the Kings of France and England for possession of Normandy embroiled the two countries in the Hundred Years' War. Despite the reinforcement of the Louvre, construction of a new encircling wall of ramparts and the Bastille, Paris was undermined by a succession of revolts and proved unable to withstand the

English. They occupied the city in 1420. Joan of Arc tried to toss them out, but in vain. England's very young Henry VI was crowned King of France in Notre-Dame in 1431. He lasted barely five years, but the patriotic French have never forgotten. A plague followed, wiping out thousands.

Renaissance and Grandeur

Paris was regarded with suspicion by the rest of the kingdom for having made peace with England's allies the Burgundians, and the city did not regain its status as capital until 1528, under François I. Palaces and mansions proliferated as the Renaissance came about and arts, science and literature flourished. A new architectural and intellectual sparkle took hold, fuelled by the growth of printing. The Louvre, originally a fortress, evolved into a royal palace, the lovely church of Saint Eustache was built, and an ornate Hôtel de Ville took over as the headquarters of municipal power.

But troubles and mass murder spoiled the charm. The Church rejected these new ideas, which they associated with the Reformation. Catholic Paris turned against its Protestants in 1572, and on August 24, in the infamous Saint Bartholomew's Day Massacre, thousands of Huguenots (Protestants) were slain. Religious wars and skirmishes continued. Paris supported the Catholic League of the Duc de Guise, whose ambition was to take the throne from Henri III. After both were killed, the legitimate heir, Henri de Navarre (crowned at Chartres as Henri IV), a Huguenot and head of the House of Bourbon, entered Paris in 1594 after renouncing his Protestant faith. "Paris is well worth a Mass", he remarked. Peace was restored by the Edict of Nantes in 1598.

Absolute Monarchy

Henry IV was a builder. Under his reign, the Pont-Neuf and the Place Royale (Place des Vosges) were constructed, the Louvre and the Tuileries extended, the marshes of the right bank built over. After his assassination in 1610, Louis XIII created the Royal Printing Press, the Jardin des Plantes, the Académie Française and by building new walls allowed the town to spread on the right bank. He also encouraged the concept of an absolute monarchy. Marie de Medici built the Luxembourg Palace in 1615. When Cardinal Mazarin ruled as regent during the minority of Louis XIV, a wave of insurrection known as the Fronde (1648–49) was the leading event. Paris was in such a state of turmoil that the court left town in 1649 to take refuge in the country.

Louis XIV always remembered this violent episode from his childhood and chose to avoid Paris, settling first in Saint-Germain, then at Versailles in 1682. The government of Paris was entrusted to Jean Baptiste Colbert, who spent his life trying to stabilize the finances of the kingdom despite the sovereign's extravagance. However, with half a million inhabitants, the capital remained the centre of the nation's intellectual life and was increasingly beautified. The colonnade of the Louvre, the Invalides (by Mansart), the Tuileries Gardens, the Gobelins workshop and the Observatory all saw the light of day, as well as several hospitals and hospices. After the king's death, a new free-

dom enveloped the city: encyclopaedists, philosophers, artists and aristocrats rejected the concept of an absolute monarchy and inaugurated the century of the Enlightenment. The intellectual élite from all of Europe converged on the cafés of the "City of Arts and Letters". Liberty, equality and national sovereignty were the burning issues of the day.

The Revolution

In 1785, the *Fermiers Généraux,* responsible for collecting the tax on goods entering Paris, built a new wall in an attempt to curb fraud.

The imposing headquarters of the mayor of Paris, built 1873–88.

The Parisians, stricken by an enduring social and economic crisis, complained bitterly. On July 14, 1789, when prices had reached an all-time high, the famished populace rose up and stormed the Bastille, confirming in blood the political revolution established a few days previously at Versailles by the declaration of the National Constituent Assembly. Concentrated in Paris, the great revolutionary events put the city at the heart of the new France. In August, the feudal system was abolished and the Declaration of the Rights of Man, based on the American declaration of 1776, was adopted. The king was brought to the Tuileries and held prisoner. Church property was nationalized in November. The following year saw the proclamation of a constitutional monarchy. But the mistakes made by Louis XVI, who tried to flee, brought about his downfall. Arrested on August 10, 1792, accused of treason and judged by the Convention, he was guillotined in January 1793 after the proclamation of the Republic.

Napoleon's Paris

Confronted by a coalition of European countries and riven by incurable internal dissension, the Revolution plunged into the Terror. In 1794, the execution of Robespierre, leader of the democrats, left the field open to the Directoire, and dreams of social revolution were extinguished.

An Englishman, Sir Richard Wallace, financed the fountains that have been providing the public with drinking water since 1872.

Five years later, a coup d'état brought to power the General Napoleon Bonaparte, hero of campaigns in Italy and Egypt. Established as First Consul, he laid the foundation for a strong state. Consecrated Emperor by the Pope in 1801, Napoleon set about leaving his mark on Paris and built the Arc de Triomphe to celebrate his military victories. The Seine was lined with embankments, the Canal de l'Ourcq was dug and drains were laid. The fall of the Empire in 1814 saw Russian and English troops encamped on the Champs-Elysées.

Paris Re-designed

The Second Empire was marked by the rise of the bourgeoisie, enriched by the Industrial Revolution, and by the suffering of a people deprived of its dreams. For several decades, Paris was to be the scene of multiple uprisings: the revolution of July 1830, riots under Louis-Philippe, until the severe suppression of the revolution of 1848. Despite its aura and its million inhabitants, Paris was still, in the middle of the 19th century, anchored in the past. In 1832, a cholera epidemic devastated the city, and in the eastern part, living conditions were deplorable. The accession to power of Napoleon III in 1851 and his policy of huge building projects was to transform the city. Under the leadership of Baron Haussmann, whole areas were demolished to give way to wide boulevards sweeping through a clean and spacious city. Bridges were built across the Seine, the sewage system modernized and a new water supply put in place. In 1860, the peripheral towns and villages were annexed and Paris was divided into 20 *arrondissements* that still have the same boundaries today.

The Second Empire ended in defeat by the Prussians. Paris, besieged and bombarded during the winter of 1870–71, repudiated the humiliating peace treaty signed by the provisional monarchist government in Versailles. The consequent uprising of the Commune and the proclamation of the Republic ended two months later in a bloodbath. Paris was burned and thousands of Parisians were either executed by firing squad or deported.

The Belle Epoque

The nation gradually recovered after the inauguration of the Third Republic. In 1876, Paris had 2 million inhabitants. Modernization of the essential services continued, opening the way to the great technical progress of the end of the century, illustrated by the series of Universal Exhibitions. The Eiffel Tower was built for the 1889 Exhibition: the Grand and Petit Palais of the Champs-Elysées and the Métro were inaugurated in 1900. A new spirit invaded the city; in the cabarets of Montmartre, Impressionist painters rubbed shoulders with poets, writers and intellectuals from all over Europe: Toulouse-Lautrec, Picasso, Van Gogh, Vlaminck, Braque, Apollinaire.

Wartime Paris

The Belle Epoque died in the trenches of World War I. The Germans were held at the Marne and never managed to take Paris. After the Armistice, the capital came alive again, and an incredible artistic and literary explosion attracted Cubists and Surrealists, Dadaists and Abstract painters. The depression of the thirties, then the outbreak of World War II, darkened the scene. Paris was occupied in June 1940 by the German Army, which stayed until the Liberation by the Allies in August 1944. These four long years of conflict were marked by curfews, raids, executions, deportations of Jews and the black market, but the city survived it all.

Paris Today

Confronted by serious housing problems in the aftermath of the war, the city embarked on modernization. In the literary cafés of Saint-Germain, writers ushered in a new era. Jazz cellars provided the background music to a period of full employment and social and economic progress which lasted until the rude awakening of May 1968 and the student riots. Street fighting and barricades made the Latin Quarter the theatre of the most recent Paris uprising to date. General de Gaulle, back in power in 1958, resigned the presidency after losing the referendum of 1969. All this time, Paris was sprouting upwards. Along the banks of the Seine, in Montparnasse and around La Défense, concrete towers were giving the city a new appearance of economic vigour. Great projects flourished, initiated by presidents wishing to leave a mark on the city: the airport at Roissy, brainchild of de Gaulle; the Georges Pompidou Centre; the Musée d'Orsay built in an old railway station and the Cité des Sciences at

La Villette blessed by Valérie Giscard d'Estaing. The great works of François Mitterand were the "New Louvre" and its glass pyramid, the Grande Arche de La Défense, the Finance Ministry at Bercy, the Bastille Opera and the new National Library of France at Tolbiac. Jacques Chirac, as mayor of Paris, had the Champs-Elysées renovated for the bicentenary of the French Revolution in 1989, and as President from 1995 to 2007 he encouraged the creation of the Musée du Quai Branly. Many other buildings and monuments have been restored since 2000, and more changes are in the works, such as the Forum des Halles and the Musée de l'Homme.

EMBELLISHING BELLEVILLE

The northeast area of Paris, stretching from the Canal de l'Ourcq to Place de la Nation, is undergoing a major facelift. It is one of the capital's most colourful districts, buzzing with life along the banks of the canal and in the neighbourhoods of the Buttes-Chaumont, Ménilmontant and Belleville. Since the 1970s, the decrepit if atmospheric buildings have been replaced by modern apartment blocks. The population has evolved into a mixture of peoples from North and West Africa and large numbers of Asians, many of them refugees from Vietnam and Cambodia, with a few irreductible Parisians still holding on around Place de Ménilmontant. Buttes-Chaumont park is a haven of greenery. Quiet streets between boulevard Sérurier and rue de Crimée are lined with charming villas and artists' studios; it feels light years away from the rest of the city. Near Père-Lachaise cemetery, the Saint-Blaise district with its church, the Charonne cemetery and its quaint old streets, is one of the last survivors of the pre-Haussmann era.

citySights

The Islands and the Seine *The origins of the capital*	20
Latin Quarter *The lively 5th arrondissement and, further south, the intriguing 13th*	28
Saint-Germain, Montparnasse *The literary districts*	36
Invalides and Eiffel Tower *Around the landmark of Paris*	46
Louvre and Palais-Royal *Memories of the monarchy*	50
Halles, Marais *Trendy yet bourgeois*	58
Bastille, Bercy, Belleville *New life in old districts*	66
Grands Boulevards *The imperial thoroughfares*	72
Champs-Elysées and the West *The world's best-known avenue and the residential 16th arrondissement*	78
Montmartre and the North *Around the Sacré-Cœur*	90
Around Paris *Castles, gardens and theme parks*	96

THE ISLANDS AND THE SEINE

The first settlement was on the Ile de la Cité, where religious, judicial and royal powers gathered from the 3rd century onwards. Linked to it by a bridge, Ile Saint-Louis is now one of the most stylish places to live.

THE DISTRICT AT A GLANCE

SIGHTS

Architecture
Notre-Dame de Paris 20
Palais de la Cité 21
Eglise Saint-Louis-en-l'Ile 22

Bridges 23

Atmosphere
Place Dauphine ★ 21

Browsing
Marché aux Fleurs/Oiseaux 21
Bouquinistes ★ 23

Treats
Berthillon ★ 22

Greenery
Square du Vert-Galant 21

WALKING TOUR 24

WINING AND DINING 102

Notre-Dame de Paris (F4) Begun in 1163 by Bishop Maurice de Sully, the Gothic cathedral was completed more than 180 years later and then restored by Viollet-le-Duc from 1845 to 1864. Stretching across the entire width of the façade, over the three main doorways, the restored Gallery of Kings consists of 28 statues representing the kings of Judah and Israel. These were pulled down during the Revolution as they were thought to be the kings of France. Inside the cathedral, admire the two huge rose windows: the 13th-century blue north window illustrates the Old Testament, whereas scenes from the New Testament are portrayed in the red south window. The towers have been newly restored. Tackle the 387 winding stairs for a close-up view of the stone gargoyles which have watched over the city for centuries. A good way to see the cathedral without the crowds is to attend an organ recital. For details see the cathedral website: www.cathedraledeparis.com • Mon–Fri 8am–6.45pm, Sat, Sun 8am–7.15pm except during services. Treasury: Mon–Sat 9.30am–6pm, Sun 1.30–6pm. Crypt: 10am–6pm (closed Mon). Towers: in summer daily 10am–

6.30pm; June–August Sat, Sun 10am–11pm; in winter daily 10am–5.30pm. Sunday mass with Gregorian chant 10am. Guided tours in English Wed, Thurs at noon, Sat 2.30pm • Parvis de Notre-Dame (4th) Ⓜ Cité ⓇⒺⓇ St-Michel ♿

Palais de la Cité (F4) Before they moved to the Louvre, the French kings ruled from the buildings that cover the western end of the Ile de la Cité, today comprising the Palais de Justice (Law Courts), Conciergerie and Sainte-Chapelle. The imposing **Conciergerie**, with slate-blue roofs and pepperpot towers, was the city's first prison and also included the living quarters of the concierge in charge of the criminals locked up there, hence its name. During the Revolution, Marie-Antoinette, Robespierre and Danton, among many thousands of political prisoners, spent their last days in its dank cells, waiting to be trundled off to the guillotine. Three 14th-century halls remain from the Capetians' palace. The first public clock in Paris can be seen on the northeast corner of the building.

The **Sainte-Chapelle** was built by Louis IX (Saint Louis) to house the Crown of Thorns and a fragment of the True Cross obtained from the emperor of Constantinople. Fifteen tall stained-glass windows form a dazzling wall of colour. The lower chapel was for the general public, the upper one for the king.

Once past the security check of the **Palais de Justice** you can mingle with barristers, witnesses, plaintiffs and reporters biding time in the splendid Salle des Pas Perdus. • Conciergerie and Sainte-Chapelle: daily, March–October 9.30am–6pm; Nov–Feb 9am–5pm. Guided tours 11am and 3pm. Palais de Justice: daily 9am–6pm • 2–4, bd du Palais (1st) Ⓜ Cité ⓇⒺⓇ St-Michel ♿

Marché aux Fleurs/Marché aux Oiseaux (F4) The flower and plant market operates daily; on Sundays exotic birds and small furry pets sold, too. • Daily 10am–7pm • Place Louis-Lépine (4th) Ⓜ Cité ⓇⒺⓇ St-Michel

Place Dauphine (F4) An elegant and tranquil triangle, created at the same time as the place des Vosges and formed by the façades of imposing 17th-century brick-walled apartment buildings. • Ile de la Cité (1st) Ⓜ Pont-Neuf

Square du Vert-Galant (F4) Henri IV the Vert-Galant ("lady-killer") was assassinated by a religious fanatic, Ravaillac. His statue watches over the little park at the tip of the island. • Ile de la Cité (1st) Ⓜ Pont-Neuf

The cathedral of Notre-Dame is one of the most popular sights on the well-beaten tourist track.

Eglise Saint-Louis-en-l'Ile (G4) Begun by Le Vau in 1664 and completed by Le Duc and Doucet in 1725, the church in the middle of the island is a masterpiece of baroque religious art, adorned with 12th-century tapestries and paintings of the Dutch, Flemish and Italian schools of the 16th and 17th centuries. • Closed Mon • 19bis, rue Saint-Louis-en-l'Ile (4th) Ⓜ Pont-Marie

Berthillon (F4) Don't leave the Ile Saint-Louis without tasting one of Berthillon's famous ice creams or sorbets. They come in every flavour imaginable, from gingerbread or licorice to marrons glacés and nougat. You can't miss the shop, there's always a queue waiting outside. And there's no need to fret if you're here in the summer when they close—many other ice cream parlours sell Berthillon specialities. • Wed–Sun 10am–8pm. Closed mid-July to end August and during school holidays, except Christmas. ☎ 01 43 54 31 61

• 29–31, rue Saint-Louis-en-l'Ile (4th) Ⓜ Pont-Marie

Bridges Following the river downstream, here are the bridges most worthy of attention.
– The **Pont de l'Archevêché** (1828) offers a striking view of Notre-Dame. It leads to Pont Saint-Louis.
– The **Pont-Neuf** (1605) was the first to be built without houses. Despite its name (*neuf* means new) it is the oldest bridge in Paris. It has been completely restored and looks as good as new.
– Pedestrians-only **Passerelle des Arts** (1804, rebuilt in steel in 1982) is furnished with benches and plants, making the view of Notre-Dame even more appealing.
– **Passerelle Solférino** (1998) makes a shortcut for pedestrians from the Tuileries to Musée d'Orsay.
– The **Pont de la Concorde** (1791) was built with stones taken from the Bastille prison.
– **Pont Alexandre III** (1900), a single steel arch, is the most romantic of the Parisian bridges, especially under the glow of its Belle Epoque lamps. The allegorical statues by Georges Récipon represent the Neva and its river nymphs.
– The **Pont de l'Alma** (1856) is known particularly for its statue of the *Zouave* by Diébolt, which acts as a gauge for the water level. A monument to Princess Diana stands at the right-bank end.
– Cross over the **Pont d'Iéna** (1913) for a good view of the Trocadéro in one direction, the Eiffel Tower and Champ de Mars in the other.
– From the **Pont Mirabeau** (1897) you can see the original Statue of Liberty, standing proudly in front of the Pont de Grenelle.

BOUQUINISTES

As you walk along the Seine, browse through the boxes of the *bouquinistes*. The name comes from *bouquin*, slang for book, but the dealers do not only dabble in second-hand and antiquarian tomes, but also old magazines, postcards, stamps, coins, engravings and posters. The tradition began in 1539, when travelling salesmen were prohibited from peddling their wares from door to door. Granted the right to sell old books in 1859, the bouquinistes enjoy a life free of bureaucratic restrictions, though regulations forbid the sale of anything lacking in "artistic merit".

WALKING TOUR: THE TWO ISLANDS

Paris's oldest bridge, the **Pont Neuf** was "new" when Henri IV inaugurated it in 1607 to join **Ile de la Cité** to the mainland. The bridge's alcoves are great for picnickers and lovers. Behind the king's statue in the middle, stairs descend to another lovers' favourite, the **Square du Vert-Galant** (Henri IV's "lady-killer" nickname) with great views of the river. Back upstairs, the king points you to the triangular **Place Dauphine**, with 17th-century redbrick and limestone houses on the two sloping sides. Along with smart restaurants and quaint tea-rooms, no. 10 was home to actors Yves Montand and Simone Signoret. Turn left on Rue de Harlay past the **Palais de Justice** courthouse and right on **Quai de l'Horloge**. Beyond the Conciergerie's pepperpot towers, where Marie-Antoinette awaited the guillotine, take Quai de la Corse to the **Marché aux Fleurs** on Place Louis-Lépine, selling flowers in beautiful glass and wrought iron halls every day, with pet birds, hamsters, rabbits and white mice on Sunday. Notice the lamposts entwined with bronze ivy! From the southwest corner, see the exquisite **Sainte-Chapelle** rising inside the Palais de Justice.

Turn left on Rue de Lutèce to **Hôtel-Dieu** hospital and right on Rue de la Cité past the **Préfecture de Police** to **Notre-Dame**, France's "parish church" (1163). On the forecourt, limestone paving traces the outline of a previous, 9th-century church. In front of Notre-Dame's main portal, a brass plate marks *Point Zéro* from which France's geographical distances are calculated. South of the Cathedral, Square Jean XXIII's shaded garden leads to the poignant World War II **Deportation Memorial**.

North of the Memorial garden, follow a pedestrian-sign over Pont Saint-Louis to **Ile Saint-Louis**. You are welcomed by a popular brasserie, ice cream parlours and cafés, almost all franchised to sell Berthillon's fabled ice cream, headquarters: 31 rue Saint-Louis-en-l'Ile, the island's main street. Its galleries, antique shops and hotels are housed in 17th-century mansions, beside the baroque **Eglise Saint-Louis-en-l'Ile**. At the far end, Le Vau's magnificent Hôtel Lambert (no. 2) is a home of the Rothschild family. Turn left on Pont de Sully for the Métro.

THE ISLANDS AND THE SEINE 25

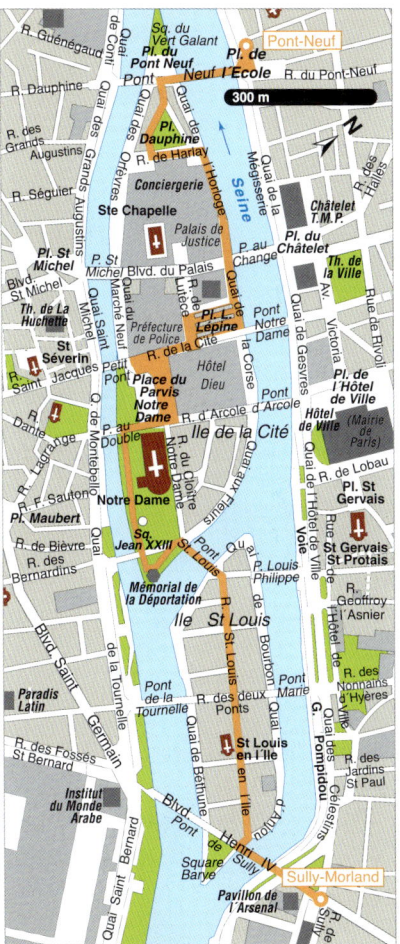

Where Paris's history began, Ile de la Cité was a royal home—and prison—beside Notre-Dame. On adjacent Ile Saint-Louis, the houses are elegant and the ice cream terrific.

Start:
Ⓜ Pont Neuf

Finish:
Ⓜ Sully Morland

CHILDREN'S PARIS

Paris has become extremely child-friendly. Practically every public garden and park now has its children's playground with sandpits, swings, roundabouts and see-saws. Most brasseries and bistros have a children's menu and, on the principle of "please the parents by keeping their kids happy," some of the smartest Michelin-starred restaurants serve Coke (*un Coca*) and tomato ketchup (*du ketchup*).

Playing in the garden
Ever since it was opened in 1860 in the northwest corner of the Bois de Boulogne, the **Jardin d'Acclimatation** has remained a children's favourite. It began as a zoo, but today the tropical beasts have gone, making way for llamas, bears and farm animals that can handle the northern climate. The variety of other attractions, such as donkey rides and boat trips, more than compensate. Access is by a little train which leaves from Porte Maillot. In the centre of town, the **Jardin des Halles** has two well-equipped children's playgrounds, one for toddlers with their parents, the other a play-jungle for the 7–11 crowd, without the parents, but with adult supervision. Check hours on tel. 01 45 08 07 18, closed Mon and in wet weather.

Puppet shows
Children don't have to understand French to be able to follow the international language of marionnette theatre—the best traditional ones are at the **Jardins du Luxembourg** (also great for sailing model boats around the fountains) **Champs-de-Mars** (ideal if the lines for the nearby Eiffel Tower are too long) and **Rond-Point des Champs-Elysées**.

Caricatures
Children love having their caricatures done—though some don't always find the result too funny. Anyway, the obvious place for this is Mont-

martre, **Place du Tertre**, but there are also the high-powered hustlers outside the **Pompidou Centre**.

Museums

Perennially popular is the waxworks at **Grévin**, 10, boulevard Montmartre, lots of lovely bloody guillotine scenes and other gore in the *horreurs* section. Parents seeking something more uplifting can head for the high-tech hands-on scientific stuff at the **Cité des Enfants** in the Cité des Sciences et de l'Industrie at La Villette. The **Palais de la Découverte** in the Grand Palais has a fine Planetarium.

Swimming

The five-storey **Aquaboulevard** (4, rue Louis-Armand, Porte de Sèvres, tel. 01 40 60 10 00) offers the biggest water sports playground in Europe in the setting of a Polynesian lagoon.

Rollerblading

An event for kids of all ages is known as Friday Night Fever in which thousands of rollerbladers skate their way in a merry but orderly procession from the south side to the north side of Paris. Except when it's too wet for safety, people usually meet up at 9.30pm near Gare Montparnasse and set out on an itinerary coordinated with the police—who have their own rollerblade patrol—details on www.pari-roller.com.

OUT OF TOWN

A couple of convenient day trips (see pp. 96–97) take you out to two theme parks, one very American, one very French. Disneyland Paris and its cinema-oriented Walt Disney Studios Park are an easy 40-minute ride on the RER's A4 line to Marne-la-Vallée. Parc Astérix, out near Roissy-Charles de Gaulle Airport, is the French counterpart devoted to the revered Gallic comic-strip heroes, Asterix, Obelix and pals. Children often find the Château de Versailles more enjoyable if you can keep them up on a summer night for the magical light shows and fireworks around the fountains and gardens.

LATIN QUARTER

The first buildings on this side of the river were abbeys. Then, in the 12th century, dissidents started teaching in the barns and stables of the Montagne Sainte-Geneviève. By 1260, there were around 60 colleges, including the one founded by Robert de Sorbon. Lessons were given in Latin, hence the name of the district. There's still something of an intellectual atmosphere in the streets around what became the Sorbonne University.

THE DISTRICT AT A GLANCE

SIGHTS

Architecture
Eglise Saint-Séverin..29
Eglise Saint-Julien-le-Pauvre.................29
Sorbonne 30
Panthéon 30
Eglise Saint-Etienne-du-Mont★...........30
Arènes de Lutèce 31
Mosquée 31
Bibliothèque nationale de France 32

Atmosphere
Place Saint-Michel............28
Quartier Saint-Séverin 29

Browsing
Shakespeare and Company................29
Marché Maubert......31
Marché Mouffetard★..........31

Museums
Musée national du Moyen Age – Thermes de Cluny★ 30
Institut du Monde arabe..........31
Muséum national d'Histoire naturelle ..32
Mobilier national – Manufacture nationale des Gobelins............32

Greenery
Musée de la Sculpture en plein air 31
Jardin des Plantes 32

WALKING TOUR 34
WINING AND DINING 102

Place Saint-Michel (F4) The square makes a good rallying point before you set out to discover the Latin Quarter. The grand fountain, by Davioud, with a bronze sculpture of St Michael killing the dragon, is surrounded by second-hand bookshops, cinemas and café terraces. To the east, wander around the pedestrian zone of the Saint-Séverin district, rue de la Huchette, rue de la Harpe, or follow the quai as far as the charming medieval rue Maître-Albert. To the west of place Saint-Michel lies another atmospheric medieval district around rue Saint-André-des-Arts, especially the gloomy passage de l'Hirondelle leading to rue Gît-le-Cœur. ⓡ St-Michel

Quartier Saint-Séverin (F4) The narrow streets of the Saint-Séverin district are packed with tourists day and night. The restaurants have names such as Naxos and Plaka, and the aroma of kebabs wafts round the corners of old houses bearing ancient shop signs. Rue de la Parcheminerie was once the street of parchment vendors and public scribes. • **Between boulevards Saint-Michel and Saint-Germain, rue Saint-Jacques and quai Saint-Michel (5th)** Ⓜ Cluny-La Sorbonne ⓡ St-Michel

Eglise Saint-Séverin (F4) A fine example of 15th-century Flamboyant Gothic architecture. In the apse, an amazing spiral column soars up to the palm-vaulted roof. See also the magnificent 14th- and 15th-century stained-glass windows. The bell in the tower is the oldest in Paris, dating from 1412. • **Mon–Sat 11am–7.30pm, Sun 11am–8pm** • **Rue des Prêtres-Saint-Séverin (5th)** Ⓜ Cluny-La Sorbonne ⓡ St-Michel

Eglise Saint-Julien-le-Pauvre (F4) The Greek catholic church of Saint-Julien-le-Pauvre was once a halt for pilgrims on the route to Santiago de Compostela. It was built in the 12th century on the site of an oratory, with stones left over from the construction of Notre-Dame. The architecture bears traces of the Romanesque style. Inside is an iconostasis dating from 1900. The locust tree shading the square outside was planted in 1602. Note the half-timbered building next door. • **Daily 9.30am–1pm and 3.30–6.30 pm** • **Square Viviani (5th)** Ⓜ Maubert-Mutualité ⓡ St-Michel

Shakespeare and Company (F4) Push open the creaky door of this legendary bookshop and browse awhile amid the shelves bulging with treasures. If you're looking for something in particular, ask the man behind the desk, he knows where everything is. The cat doesn't mind being stroked. • **Daily from noon to midnight or thereabouts** • **37, rue de la Bûcherie (5th)** Ⓜ Maubert-Mutualité

Musée national du Moyen Age – Thermes de Cluny (F5) Beside the remains of the Gallo-Roman thermal baths, a 15th-century mansion housing a marvellous collection of medieval sculpture, illuminated manuscripts, stained glass, bronzes and tapestries—of which the highlight is the intriguing series depicting *The Lady and the Unicorn*. Round the back, in the Square de Cluny, see the medieval garden, and don't miss the beautiful sculpted staircase beneath the chapel. • **Daily (except Tues and holidays) 9.15am–5.45pm. Garden: daily, summer 8am–9.30pm, winter 9am–5.30pm. Terrace: 9.15am–5.45pm** • 6, pl. Paul-Painlevé (5th) Ⓜ Cluny-La Sorbonne Ⓡ St-Michel

Sorbonne (F5) Robert de Sorbon, the chaplain of Louis IX, founded the university in 1257 as a college for impoverished theological students. Richelieu, who financed reconstruction in 1642, is buried in the chapel (closed to the public). You can see the grand amphitheatre, with its statues of Richelieu, Sorbon, Descartes and Pascal, and a huge allegorical painting by Puvis de Chavannes on the back wall. • **Visits by appointment only, for groups of min. 10 and max. 30; call the Rectorat,** ☎ 01 40 46 23 49 • Place de la Sorbonne (5th); boutique 17, rue de la Sorbonne Ⓡ Luxembourg

Panthéon (F5) The church designed by Soufflot for Louis XV was turned into a mausoleum during the Revolution. Among the great Frenchmen resting there are Voltaire, Rousseau, Victor Hugo and Jean Moulin. The nave (where you can watch Foucault's pendulum oscillating) and crypt are open to the public, and you can climb up to the dome for a spectacular view. • **Daily, summer 10am–6.45pm, winter 10am–5.15pm. Closed on public holidays** • Place du Panthéon (5th) Ⓜ Cardinal-Lemoine Ⓡ Luxembourg

Eglise Saint-Etienne-du-Mont (F5) Behind the Pantheon and next to the Lycée Henri IV, a famous high school, this church has been beautifully renovated. Its façade is composed of three superposed pediments in different styles. Inside is the shrine of St Genevieve, and the only surviving rood screen *(jubé)* in Paris, dating from the 16th century. • **Mon noon–7.30pm, Tues–Fri 8.45am–7.30pm (closed during school holidays); Sat 8.45am–noon and 2–7.30pm, Sun 8.45am–12.15pm and 2.30–7.30pm** • 1, place Sainte-Geneviève (5th) Ⓜ Maubert-Mutualité

Marché Maubert (F5) Good open-air food market with a village-like atmosphere. • Tues, Thurs 7am–2.30pm, Sat 7am–3pm • Place Maubert (5th) Ⓜ Maubert-Mutualité

Arènes de Lutèce (F5) The ancient amphitheatre is the only Parisian monument remaining from Gallo-Roman times, apart from the Baths of Cluny. It is now enclosed by imposing apartment buildings, and the local children play football in the arena. • **Daily, summer 8am–10 pm, winter 8am–5pm** • 47, rue Monge (5th) Ⓜ Jussieu

Mosquée (F5) The Great Mosque was built from 1922 to 1926 in "hispano-mauresque" style with marble colonnade, mosaic friezes and a minaret 33 m (108 ft) high. Sample mint tea and Arab pastries in the tearoom or enjoy a steam bath in the hammam. • **Daily (except Fri) 9am–noon and 2–6pm. Guided tours.** • Place du Puits-de-l'Ermite (5th), entrance to the hammam at 39, rue Geoffroy-Saint-Hilaire Ⓜ Place Monge

Marché Mouffetard (F5) On ancient maps of Paris, rue Mouffetard meanders far out into the countryside—it was the old Roman road leading to Rome. The street still has a typical village-like character, with a market every morning, some interesting façades, and lots of cafés and tiny restaurants (you may have seen one in the film *Amélie*). • **Every morning except Mon** • Rue Mouffetard (5th) Ⓜ Place Monge

Institut du Monde arabe (G5) Art and literature of the Arab world from the 8th to 19th centuries, in an ultra-modern glass and aluminium building. The windows open and close automatically with the variation in light, like a camera shutter. Superb views from the restaurant on the roof terrace. • **Daily (except Mon) 10am–6pm** • 1, rue des Fossés-St-Bernard (5th) Ⓜ Jussieu Cardinal-Lemoine Ⓡ Gare d'Austerlitz ♿

Musée de la Sculpture en plein air (G5) Contemporary sculpture is displayed on a two-year rotation basis in this little park on the banks of the Seine. • **Open day and night; free admission** • Quai Saint-Bernard (5th) Ⓡ Gare d'Austerlitz

Jardin des Plantes (G5) The Royal Garden of Medicinal Plants was set up during the reign of Louis XII. In 1793 the museum and menagerie were created, but many of the animals were killed and eaten during the siege of Paris in 1870. The botanical garden has formal flower beds, alpine and Mediterranean gardens, roses, irises and tropical plants. • **Open daily from sunrise to sunset.** Menagerie 9am–5pm. Greenhouses closed for renovation. Bookshop daily (except Tues) 10am–6pm. • Entrance place Valhubert, rue Buffon, rue Geoffroy-Saint-Hilaire or rue Cuvier (5th) Ⓜ Gare d'Austerlitz, Jussieu ♿

Muséum national d'Histoire naturelle (F–G5) The Natural History Museum is divided into several sections: mineralogy and geology (meteorites); paleontology (dinosaur skeletons); anatomy; and the department of evolution. The glass and cast-iron **Grande Galerie de l'Evolution** contains a splendid collection of rare or extinct species. Temporary exhibitions. • Grande Galerie: daily (except Tues) 10am–6pm. Galeries de Paléontologie and Galerie de Minéralogie: daily (except Tues) 10am–5pm • 57, rue Cuvier and 36, rue Geoffroy-Saint-Hilaire (5th) Ⓜ Censier-Daubenton Ⓡ Gare d'Austerlitz ♿

Bibliothèque nationale de France (G6) President Mitterrand replaced the grand old Bibliothèque nationale in rue Richelieu by this new glass library. The design by Dominique Perrault represents four open books. • Mon 2–7pm, Tues–Sat 9am–7pm, Sun 1pm–7pm. Closed on public holidays. ☎ 01 53 79 59 59 • 11 quai François-Mauriac (13th) Ⓜ Bibliothèque F. Mitterrand ♿

Mobilier national – Manufacture nationale des Gobelins (F6) Colbert created the Manufacture in 1662, to bring together several small Parisian tapestry workshops. They included that of the Gobelin family, who had been dyeing crimson on this site near the Bièvre river since the 15th century. Temporary exhibitions are held in the Galerie des Gobelins. • Gallery: daily (except Mon) during exhibitions 12.30–6.30pm. Workshops: guided tours (French only, tickets sold at FNAC, ☎ 08 92 68 46 94, or on the spot 15 min before tour): Tues, Wed, Thurs 2 and 3pm (including Gallery tour during exhibitions). Groups by reservation on ☎ 01 40 13 46 46 • 42, av. des Gobelins (13th) Ⓜ Gobelins

SOUP FOR THE SOUL

After a hard morning's sightseeing, there's nothing more invigorating than to find a seat in a cosy bistro, preferably with a good view of the passers-by, and to enjoy a steaming dish of *soupe à l'oignon* with a glass of red wine. This is one Parisian flavour you will be able to recreate for yourself back home.

Originally, the word *soupe* referred to a slice of bread, upon which a liquid—sauce, wine or stock—was poured, and French onion soup is a call-back to those distant times. Nowadays, *soupe* is synonymous with *potage*, and generally describes a thin soup embellished with pasta, rice, vegetables, meat or fish.

There are hundreds of recipes for French onion soup. This one is easy and quite tasty.

Soupe à l'oignon for 6 servings
butter for frying
250 g (8 oz) onions, finely chopped
25 g (scant 1 oz) flour
2 litres (4 pints) stock (you can replace half a litre of stock with dry white wine)
2 tbsp port
thick slices of bread
grated cheese such as cheddar (optional)

Melt the butter in a saucepan and fry the onions gently until golden, without letting them brown. Sprinkle with the flour and stir with a wooden spoon for a few minutes. Pour in the wine and stock and bring to the boil. Turn down the heat, add the port, leave to simmer for 30 minutes. Toast the slices of bread or dry them in the oven. Place a slice of bread in the bottom of each dish, pour the hot soup over, and sprinkle with grated cheese.

WALKING TOUR: RUE MOUFFETARD, "LA MOUFFE"

At **Place Saint-Michel**, turn into narrow pedestrian **Rue de la Huchette**, lined with Greek and Asian restaurants and tourist shops, busy day and night. Shake off the runners who will grab you by the arm to drag you into their restaurants and wander off into the side streets, some of the oldest in Paris. If you walk right to the end of Rue de la Huchette, cross over the road to **Rue de la Bûcherie**, site of the famous Shakespeare and Company bookshop. Note, however, that this is not the original shop and lending library founded by Sylvia Beach, which was in Rue de l'Odéon in the Saint-Germain district.

Past the shop, turn into Rue Saint-Julien-le-Pauvre. Go around the church and head towards **Place Maubert**. This is like any typical French village square, surrounded by food shops and colonized by a lively market Tuesday, Thursday and Saturday mornings. From the corner of the square, walk up the long and narrow **Rue de la Montagne-Sainte-Geneviève**, which passes on one side the Ecole Polytechnique. Call in at the lovely church of **Saint-Etienne-du-Mont**, then carry on straight up **Rue Descartes** where the poet Paul Verlaine lived at no. 39 (on the way, look out on the right for the Tour Clovis remaining from Philippe Auguste's city wall). Straight ahead is the picturesque **Place de la Contrescarpe** with two popular cafés. If you are lucky, you may find an empty table outside, an excellent vantage point for people-watching and drinking in the atmosphere. Hemingway lived just round the corner on Rue du Cardinal Lemoine; he wrote about this square in *The Snows of Kilimanjaro*. Look up at the unusual sign on the building on the right-hand side of the square—*Au Nègre Joyeux*, painted in 1748. Stroll along **Rue Mouffetard**, taking time to peep into the little shops, listen to the stall-holders' incomprehensible banter, and watch the locals prodding cheeses, sniffing mushrooms and inspecting the fish. At no. 6, note the 18th-century bas-relief of two golden oxen, a reminder of the times when tanners and tripe butchers worked in the area. At the far end of the street stands the church of **Saint-Médard**, surrounded by trees and flowerbeds.

If you want to stop your walk here, turn left at the end of the street, turn left into Rue Daubenton and catch the métro at Censier.

QUARTIER LATIN 35

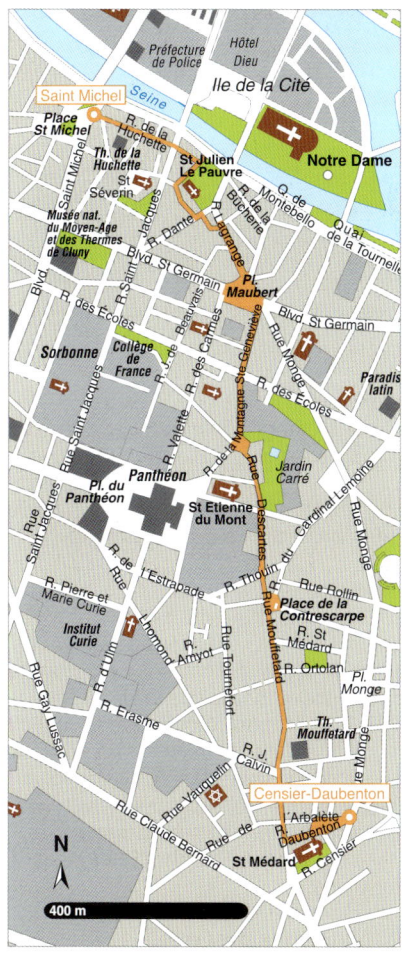

Deep below the cobbles of Rue Mouffetard lie the stones of the old Roman road from Paris to Rome.

Start:
Ⓜ Saint-Michel

Finish:
Ⓜ Censier-Daubenton

Outdoor market on rue Mouffetard closed Mondays

36 CITYSIGHTS

SAINT-GERMAIN, MONTPARNASSE

When Louis XI decided to leave the Louvre and take the court to Versailles, the aristocrats moved to the left bank, settling in the suburb of Saint-Germain, on the road to Versailles. Around a hundred superb mansions still exist to this day on rue de Grenelle and rue de Varenne, including the Palais Bourbon (seat of the National Assembly) and the Hôtel Matignon, official residence of the Prime Minister. Further south, Montparnasse, the haunt of poets, singers and philosphers up to the 1930s, clusters around a high tower. Now a largely commercial and residential area, it has undergone drastic changes in recent years, though you can still see some artists' studios in Art Nouveau and Art Deco style.

THE DISTRICT AT A GLANCE

SIGHTS

Architecture
Eglise Saint-Sulpice ..38
Eglise Saint-Germain-des-Prés 39
Institut de France 40
Basilique Sainte-Clotilde..........42
La Pagode 42
Tour Montparnasse..42

Atmosphere
Saint-Germain-des-Prés★ 37
Odéon....................38

Cimetière du Montparnasse 43
Rue de la Gaîté.........43
Catacombes 43

Browsing
Marché Saint-Germain 38
Carré Rive Gauche ...40
Le Bon Marché 42
Marché biologique...43

Museums
Musée du Luxembourg 38
Observatoire 38
Musée Zadkine 38
Musée Delacroix 39

Musée de la Monnaie 40
Musée d'Orsay★......40
Musée de la Légion d'Honneur 41
Musée Maillol..........41
Musée Rodin★ 42
Musée Bourdelle......43
Fondation Cartier.....43

Greenery
Jardins du Luxembourg 37
Parc Montsouris.......43

WALKING TOUR 44

WINING AND DINING 103

Jardins du Luxembourg (E5) Beautifully dressed French children sail their little boats on the pond in this formal garden, where mossy statues drowse beneath chestnut trees, students ponder the meaning of life between lectures and lovers meet beside the large Medicis fountain created in the 17th century. Wandering around the gravel paths, you will see vegetable gardens and an orchard, orchids and beehives (the autumn harvest is sold in the Orangerie), tennis courts, playgrounds and puppet shows. Statues of angels, cherubs, historical and mythical figures and animals are scattered here and there beneath the foliage. • Bd Saint-Michel (6th) Ⓡ Luxembourg

SAINT-GERMAIN-DES-PRÉS

Cinemas, designer boutiques, cafés and bookshops are all hallmarks of boulevard Saint-Germain, at its most lively around the old church of the same name. The romantic, literary aura of the Saint-Germain of the 1950s has all but disappeared. Strolling through the narrow streets between the boulevard and the river—rues de Seine, Saint-André-des-Arts, de l'Echaudé, Christine, place Furstenberg—you'll sense the rare, authentic "Parisian" atmosphere. Between boulevard Saint-Germain (opposite the statue of Danton, his arm outstretched towards the Latin Quarter) and rue Saint-André-des-Arts, the cobbled Cour du Commerce Saint-André is lined with 18th-century houses. Peep through the windows of the building opposite Procope to see a vestige of Philippe-Auguste's city wall; on the same side, don't miss the succession of picturesque, leafy courtyards; one of them still has an old mounting block by the gate. Walk through them to reach rue du Jardinet, a short-cut to the rue de l'Eperon.

Musée du Luxembourg (E5) The Orangerie of the Senate has been transformed into a museum that organizes prestigious exhibitions. • Mon, Fri, Sat 10.30am–10pm, Tues–Thurs 10.30am–7pm, Sun and holidays 9.30am–7pm ☏ 01 42 34 25 95 • 19, rue de Vaugirard (6th) Ⓜ Odéon Ⓡ Luxembourg

Observatoire de Paris (E6) This observatory, built by Claude Perrault in the 17th century, is the oldest in the world still in activity. To see the magnificent collection of astronomical instruments, you will have to send a written request enclosing a self-addressed envelope to the Service des Visites. • 61, av. de l'Observatoire (6th) Ⓜ Denfert-Rochereau

Musée Zadkine (E5) A marvellous museum displaying 300 wood, bronze and stone works by the Russian sculptor Ossip Zadkine, in the studio that he occupied from 1928 until his death in 1967. Some of the sculptures are described in Braille panels, and blind people can touch some of the pieces. There's also a peaceful garden. Temporary exhibitions of the work of contemporary artists are presented in the workshop. • Daily (except Mon and public holidays) 10am–6pm • 100bis, rue d'Assas (6th) Ⓜ Notre-Dame des Champs ♿

Eglise Saint-Sulpice (E4) The great white church has strange, unmatching towers—the work of two different architects. The walls and ceiling of the Chapelle des Saints-Anges, to the right of the entrance, are decorated with frescoes painted by Delacroix between 1853 and 1861. A curiosity of the church is the gnomon, on the left-hand side, near the altar. A little diagram explains how this marble obelisk and its brass marker are supposed to measure noon.
• Daily 7.30am–7.15pm • Place Saint-Sulpice (6th) Ⓜ St-Sulpice

Odéon (E4–5) With its cafés, cinemas and boutiques, the area between the boulevard and the neoclassical Odéon theatre, built in 1779 and undergoing renovation, is one of the liveliest in Paris. • Bd Saint-Germain (6th) Ⓜ Odéon

Marché Saint-Germain (E4) Inaugurated in 1818 on the site of the Saint-Germain fair, this neat arcaded building houses a pristine covered market and rather chic shopping mall, a swimming pool and a car park. • Market: Tues–Sat

In the little park next to the church of Saint-Germain, Picasso's bronze statue of Dora Maar is dedicated to the poet Guillaume Apollinaire.

8am–1pm and 4–8pm, Sun 8am–1pm; boutiques: Mon–Sat 10am–7.30pm • 3ter, rue Mabillon (6th) Ⓜ Mabillon

Eglise Saint-Germain-des-Prés (E4) This parish church, with a rather plain exterior and gloomy interior, was begun in the year 1000 on the site of an abbey destroyed by the Vikings. Little is left of the original. The walls and columns are covered in polychrome painting. In the choir, see the tombstones of Descartes (right-hand side) and Boileau (on the left). Parisians meet up or enjoy a lunchtime sandwich in the park next to the church, around Picasso's monument to Apollinaire, on the site of the old cloisters. • Mon–Sat 8am–8pm, Sun 9am–8pm • 3, place Saint-Germain (6th) Ⓜ St-Germain-des-Prés

Musée national Eugène Delacroix (E4) A collection of sketches and drawings by the painter in his last abode; you can also visit his studio, which has some of his personal belongings and a few paintings. Delacroix's works are all

over Paris: in the Louvre, Musée d'Orsay, Musée des Arts décoratifs, Musée Carnavalet, Musée de la Vie romantique, and the churches of Saint-Paul Saint-Louis (4th), Saint-Denis-du-Saint-Sacrement (3rd) and Saint-Sulpice (6th).
• Daily (except Tues) 9.30am–5pm (last tickets at 4.30pm) • 6, rue de Furstenberg (6th) Ⓜ St-Germain-des-Prés

Musée de la Monnaie (E4) This neoclassical building, inaugurated in 1771, was the French Mint for 200 years. Today it houses a museum of coins and medals, tracing the history of France from antiquity to modern times. You can also see the old presses. The boutique sells jewellery in gold, silver and bronze, medals, replicas of ancient coins, and so on. • Daily (except Mon and public holidays) 11am–5.30pm, Sat, Sun noon–5.30pm • 11, quai de Conti (6th) Ⓜ Pont Neuf

Institut de France (E4) Since the Revolution, the former Four-Nations college (1691), financed by Mazarin, has housed the seat of the French Academy. The august members, called the Immortals, are the ultimate authority on the French language, and meet weekly to compile a dictionary. Beneath its dome, the building also houses the Mazarine Library, the first public library in France, now reserved for professionals. • Guided tours Sat, Sun and public holidays at 3pm • 23, quai de Conti (6th) Ⓜ Pont Neuf, St-Germain

Carré Rive Gauche (E4) Collectors come from all over the world to visit the 123 galleries and antique shops in the block of streets bounded by quai Voltaire, rues du Bac, des Saints-Pères and de l'Université. Fascinating for window-shopping, too. The site was originally the garden of Queen Margot.
• Rue du Bac (7th) Ⓜ Rue du Bac

Musée d'Orsay (E4) The building was originally a railway station, inaugurated in 1900 for the World's Fair and listed as a historic monument in 1978. Transforming it into a museum was one of the most brilliant ideas of the end of the 20th century. The architecture alone is enough to take your breath away. You'll need at least three hours to see the best of the magnificent collections covering the evolution of French art from 1848 to 1914: Impressionists and post-Impressionists, Art Nouveau furniture, sculpture, architecture, the beginnings of photography. Pick up a plan at the entrance as it isn't too easy to find your way around. The Impressionists are on the top floor, reached by escalators hidden by great pillars at the far end of the main hall. The restaurant, on the middle level above the entrance, is rather grand, all gold trim and chandeliers. There's a more easy-going Rooftop Café on the upper level, with an outside terrace. • **Daily (except Mon) 9.30am–6pm, Thurs late closing 9.45pm. Advance entry tickets are sold in the kiosk outside, Tues–Fri 9.30am–5pm (Thurs till 9pm)** ☎ 01 40 49 48 14 • 1, rue de la Légion d'Honneur (7th) Ⓜ Solférino ⓇⒺⓇ Musée d'Orsay ♿

Musée de la Légion d'Honneur et des Ordres de Chevalerie (D4) The superbly renovated museum in the Hôtel de Salm traces the history of distinguished French and foreign awards such as the Legion of Honour and the Order of the Garter, from the times of Louis XI to the present, and recounts the lives of illustrious recipients. • **Wed–Sun 1–6pm, Tues groups only** ☎ 01 40 62 84 25 • 2, rue de la Légion d'Honneur (7th) Ⓜ Solférino ⓇⒺⓇ Musée d'Orsay

Musée Maillol (D5) Dina Vierny (1919–2009) worked as a model for Maillol, and the museum she founded, in the Hôtel de Bouchardon (at one time the home of Alfred de Musset) is dedicated to the sculptor's work. It also includes paintings by Matisse, Pougny, Poliakoff and others, and holds temporary exhibitions. • **Daily (except Tues and public holidays) 11am–6pm; ticket office closes at 5.15pm** • 59–61, rue de Grenelle (7th) Ⓜ Rue du Bac ♿

ANTIQUES

Whether you're a discriminating amateur of Boulle commodes or an inveterate collector of kitsch, you're bound to find something tantalizing in the hundreds of antique shops. The more expensive businesses are grouped around Faubourg Saint-Honoré, Faubourg Saint-Germain (rues de Seine, Jacob, des Saints-Pères, Bonaparte), in the Marais (village Saint-Paul) and around the Pompidou Centre. Savvy collectors go to the daily auctions at the Hôtel Drouot, see www.drouot.fr

Musée Auguste Rodin (D4) The large and elegant 18th-century Hôtel Biron provides the perfect setting for some of Rodin's finest sculptures, which he donated to the State. The sculptor lived here when the house was transformed into apartments for artists—other famous residents were the German poet Rainer Maria Rilke, Isadora Duncan, Cocteau and Matisse. On the ground floor, a room is reserved for the works of Rodin's student, model and mistress, Camille Claudel. The museum includes paintings from Rodin's personal collection (by Van Gogh, Renoir, Monet and so on). His famous *Le Penseur* (The Thinker), the *Bourgeois de Calais,* the *Porte de l'Enfer* and *Balzac* are set in the grounds. There's a café-restaurant on the west side of the garden; on the opposite side is the Marble Gallery. • **Daily (except Mon), summer 9.30am–5.45pm, winter 9.30am–4.45pm** • **77, rue de Varenne (7th)** Ⓜ **Varenne** ⓇⒺⓇ **Invalides** ♿

Basilique Sainte-Clotilde (D4) Imposing neo-Gothic parish church with fine stained-glass windows. Opposite, the small Samuel-Rousseau Square is planted with chestnut, judas and Japanese pagoda (or scholar) trees. • **23bis, rue Las Cases (7th)** Ⓜ **Assemblée nationale, Solférino**

Le Bon Marché Rive Gauche (D–E4) The first department store in Paris was founded by Aristide Boucicaut in 1852 and designed by Gustave Eiffel. Boucicaut had a statue erected in the park opposite the store, representing his wife dispensing charity. Don't miss the food department (Grande Epicerie de Paris, magasin 2, ground floor), Mon–Sat 8.30am–9pm. Good cooked foods (service traiteur). • **Mon–Wed 10am–7.30pm, Thurs 10am–9pm, Fri 10am–8pm, Sat 9.30am–8pm** • **38, rue de Sèvres (7th)** Ⓜ **Sèvres-Babylone**

La Pagode (D4) This authentic Japanese pagoda, a historic monument, is actually a cinema, with an excellent programme. • **57bis, rue de Babylone (7th)** Ⓜ **Saint-François-Xavier**

Tour Montparnasse (D5) A lift whisks you up in 38 seconds to the 56th floor for one of the best views over Paris, with viewpoint tables to help you locate the city's monuments. The exhibition includes photo galleries, interactive screens, multimedia presentations on the history and symbolism of various towers around the world. There are also quizzes, video clips and more. The tower was built in 1973. Panoramic roof terrace on the 59th floor, with a view stretching up to 40 km (25 miles). • **Daily, summer 9.30am–11.30pm, winter 9.30am–10.30pm** (t9.30am–11 pm Fri, Sat and evenings before bank holidays) • Rue de l'Arrivée (15th) Ⓜ Montparnasse-Bienvenüe ♿

Musée Bourdelle (D5) Works by the sculptor Bourdelle, displayed in his house, studio and garden. The exhibition space has been extended by the architect Portzamparc. • **Daily (except Mon and public holidays) 10am–6pm** • 18, rue Antoine-Bourdelle (15th) Ⓜ Falguière ♿

Rue de la Gaîté (D5) A colourful and lively street lined with theatres, cabarets, cinemas and cafés. Ⓜ Gaîté

Marché biologique (E5) Organic produce is sold on the boulevard between rue de Cherche-Midi and rue de Rennes. • **Sun 9am–2pm** • Bd Raspail (6th) Ⓜ Rennes

Cimetière du Montparnasse (D–E6) Among the distinguished residents of this peaceful cemetery lie the writers Maupassant, Baudelaire, Simone de Beauvoir and Jean-Paul Sartre. • **Daily, summer 8am–6pm, winter 8am–5.30pm** • Bd Edgar-Quinet (14th) Ⓜ Edgar-Quinet, Raspail

Fondation Cartier (E6) Designed by Jean Nouvel, the steel and glass building is used for high-quality modern art exhibitions (painting, sculpture, fashion, and so on). • **Tues 11am–10pm, Wed, Sun 11am–8pm** • 261, bd Raspail (14th) Ⓜ Raspail Ⓜ ⓇⒺⓇ Denfert-Rochereau ♿

Catacombes (E6) A grisly tour through an ancient quarry transformed into a huge underground cemetery containing the skeletons of 6 million Parisians. • **Daily (except Mon) 10am–5pm** • 1, place Denfert-Rochereau (14th) Ⓜ ⓇⒺⓇ Denfert-Rochereau

Parc Montsouris (off map, dir. E6) Near the university campus, the hilly park was created by Baron Haussmann. Relaxed atmosphere, grotto, waterfall, statues and majestic trees. • Bd Jourdan (14th) ⓇⒺⓇ Cité Universitaire ♿

WALKING TOUR: MONTPARNASSE, SAINT-GERMAIN

At the intersection of **Boulevard Montparnasse** and Boulevard Raspail, now aptly named Place Pablo Picasso, are cafés and restaurants where the artist met fellow painters and writers: the Dôme, La Coupole, La Rotonde and Le Sélect, closest in atmosphere to the easy-going haunts of the 1920s. Just north on Boulevard Raspail is Rodin's massive bronze statue of Balzac. Behind him, turn right on **Rue Vavin** across Rue Notre-Dame-des-Champs to no. 26 where architect Henri Sauvage's white ceramic-tiled building (1912) is a fine French example of the Modern Movement.

Porte Vavin entrance to the **Jardins du Luxembourg** leads to the gardens' pagoda-like hives where 1,000,000 bees make honey (sold from September at the Orangerie near the Senate). Left past the *boulodrome*, head for the small-scale Statue of Liberty, beside an oak planted by local Americans for victims of September 11, 2001, "as a symbol of Franco-American friendship". At Porte Fleurus, literary pilgrims make a detour to **27, rue Fleurus** where writer Gertrude Stein hosted Hemingway, Scott Fitzgerald and Picasso. Back in the gardens, circle poet Paul Verlaine's monument, past a tipsy bronze of Silenus, teacher and companion of wine-god Dionysus, and exit at the northwest gate.

Across Rue Vaugirard, take the short tree-lined Allée du Séminaire over to **Place Saint-Sulpice**. With its big church, four bishops on its fountain and seminary (now disused), the square became a symbol of religiosity, *saint-sulpiceries* being shops that sell religious artefacts. From Café de la Mairie's terrace, watch the neighbourhood's pagan fashion victims.

Or follow them to designer boutiques on **Rue Bonaparte** and right on **Rue du Four**. Make a side-trip on Rue Princesse to the English-language bookshop Village Voice and British sports pub, Frog and Princess. Back across Rue du Four, the narrow Rue des Ciseaux takes you to **Boulevard Saint-Germain** and the south side of the great Romanesque church. The square in front of the church is now Place Sartre-Beauvoir, honouring the high priest and priestess of **Saint-Germain-des-Prés** intellectuals. They met their groupies at the two cafés, *Deux Magots* and *Flore*, around the corner from the jazz clubs on **Rue Saint-Benoît**.

SAINT-GERMAIN, MONTPARNASSE 45

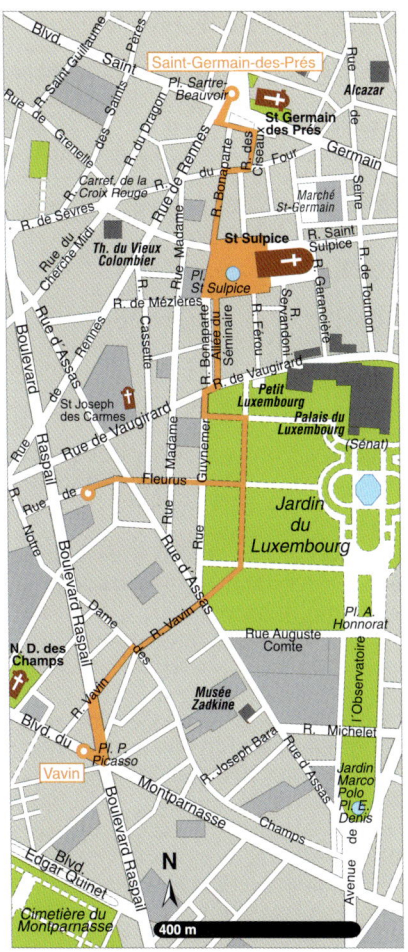

The Left Bank haunts of writers and artists from both sides of the Atlantic extend through the backstreets and gardens between boulevards Montparnasse and Saint-Germain.

Start:
Ⓜ Vavin

Finish:
Ⓜ Saint-Germain-des-Prés

INVALIDES AND THE EIFFEL TOWER

Take a walk along the quays past the columns and classical façade of the National Assembly, to reach the Invalides, visible from afar with its golden dome. Louis XIV founded the Invalides as the first national hospital for soldiers wounded in action. If you feel up to walking further, you will eventually reach the Eiffel Tower at the end of the Champ-de-Mars, facing the Trocadéro on the other side of the Seine.

THE DISTRICT AT A GLANCE

SIGHTS	**Museums** Hôtel national des Invalides..................46	**Greenery** Parc André-Citroën★.......47
Architecture Eiffel Tower★...........47	Musée des Egouts....46	WALKING TOUR 48
Browsing Village suisse...........47	Musée du quai Branly.....................47	WINING AND DINING 104

Hôtel national des Invalides (D4) Built in the 17th century, the Invalides is one of the most prestigious monuments of the capital. The majestic façade was designed by Libéral Bruant. The complex incorporates the church of Saint-Louis, built at the end of the 18th century, and several museums documenting the Army, the Order of Liberation, the audiovisual **Historial Charles de Gaulle**, and Relief Maps (scale models of fortified French towns). You can also see **Napoleon's Tomb**: the emperor reposes in an ornate wooden coffin beneath the great golden dome. • Daily (except first Mon of month), summer 10am–6pm, winter 10am–5pm, Tues till 9pm • Esplanade des Invalides (7th) Ⓜ Varenne Ⓡ Invalides

Musée des Egouts (C3) A visit of the sewers through specially built galleries, and a fascinating audio-visual show tracing their history, from the first tunnels dug out in 1370 to today's modern system. • Daily (except Thurs and Fri), summer 11am–5pm, winter 11am–4pm ☎ 01 53 68 27 81 • Opposite 93,

INVALIDES AND EIFFEL TOWER

quai d'Orsay (7th) Ⓜ Alma-Marceau Ⓡ Pont de l'Alma

Musée du quai Branly (C3) Designed by Jean Nouvel, the museum displays the arts and culture of every continent but Europe, including masks, costumes, textiles, musical instruments. An outside wall, the Mur végétal, is covered with over 15,000 plants of 150 species. • Tues, Wed, Sun 11am–7pm, Thurs–Sat 11am–9pm. Closed May 1, Dec 25 ☎ 01 56 61 71 72 • Entrances 27, 37, 51 quai Branly, 206, 218 rue de l'Université; wheelchair access at no. 222 (7th) Ⓜ Pont de l'Alma Ⓡ Champ-de-Mars ♿

Eiffel Tower (C4) The highlight of the 1889 World's Fair has become the symbol of Paris. The tower has restaurants and tea-rooms on the two lower platforms and a lookout on the third with a view reaching 43 miles (70 km) on a clear day. • Daily, Jan–mid-June 9.30am–11.45pm by the elevators (last lift to top 10.30pm); mid-June–end August 9am–midnight (last lift 11 pm); Sept–Dec 9.30am–11.45pm (last lift 11pm). Last entry to stairs 6.30pm ☎ 01 44 11 23 23 • Champ-de-Mars (7th) Ⓜ Bir-Hakeim Ⓡ Champ-de-Mars ♿

Village suisse (C4) A hundred antique dealers in the Swiss Pavilion of the 1889 World's Fair. • Thurs–Mon 10.30am–7pm • 78, av. de Suffren (15th) Ⓜ La Motte-Picquet-Grenelle

Parc André-Citroën (B5) Orange grove, white garden, black garden, and Mediterranean flora. • Rue Balard (15th) Ⓜ Balard

The ornate bridge named after Tsar Alexander III links the Invalides on the left bank with the Grand Palais on the right.

WALKING TOUR: CHAMP-DE-MARS – INVALIDES

Head west on Avenue La Motte-Picquet to the 18th-century **Ecole Militaire** and the equestrian statue of Marshal Joffre inscribed with optimistic declarations of September 1914. In front of what is now the Ecole Supérieure de Guerre (War College) behind him, he points with his baton to a handsome modern **Mur pour la Paix** (Wall for Peace, 2001) by Jean-Michel Wilmotte and Clara Halter. The word "peace" is written on walls and pillars of glass and Hiroshima granite in 32 languages and 14 alphabets.

Continue north across the **Champ de Mars**. Transformed from 16th-century vineyards for military manoeuvres and parades, the Field of Mars is now a public park, with a children's playground over to the left and a marionnette theatre to the right. Of the temporary monuments built for five world fairs on this vast field between 1867 and 1937, just the **Eiffel Tower** (1889) remains stubbornly behind.

Exit the Champ de Mars on the right along Avenue Barbey-d'Aurevilly to cross Place de Général-Gouraud, and continue on **Avenue Rapp** into the heart of the *grand bourgeois* 7th's lofty apartment buildings. The most distinguished is at no. 29, an Art Nouveau signed masterpiece by Jules Lavirotte (1901). Double back and turn into **Square Rapp** where Lavirotte has another flamboyant building at no. 3.

Back on Place Général-Gouraud, turn left on **Rue Saint-Dominique** with its smart boutiques and a nice street fountain at no. 131. Continue across Avenue Bosquet to turn right on **Rue Cler** to its lively street-market (some stalls close Monday) in the pedestrian zone beyond Rue de Grenelle. Double back and turn on right on Rue de Grenelle. Through an archway opposite Eglise Saint-Jean, Passage Jean-Nicot (who in 1560 introduced tobacco, whence *nicotine*) leads to Rue Jean-Nicot. At the far end is the impressive **Conservatoire Erik Satie** (131bis rue de l'Université, 1983) by Christian Portzamparc, architect of the Cité de la Musique.

Rue de l'Université leads to the huge **Esplanade des Invalides**, where Napoleon placed St Mark's Lion, stolen from Venice in 1797 (and returned in 1815).

INVALIDES AND EIFFEL TOWER   49

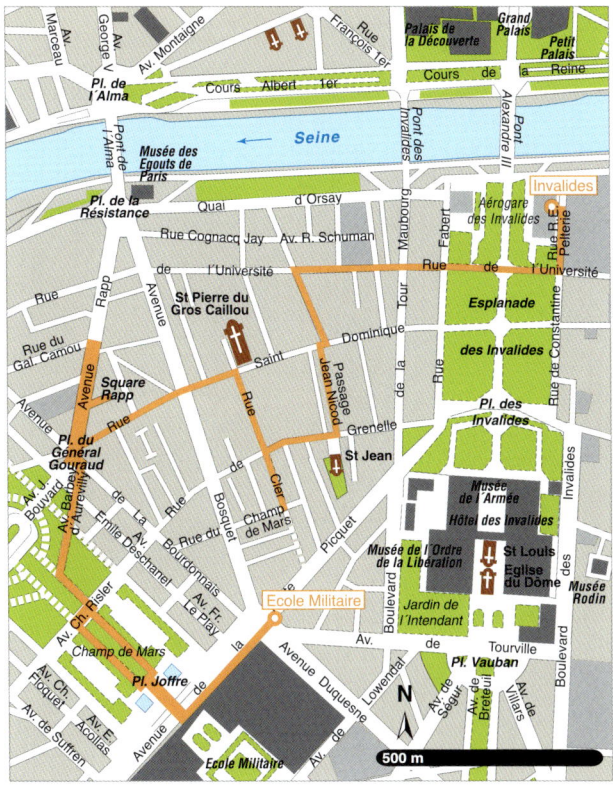

From the Ecole Militaire to the old soldiers' Invalides, the 7th arrondissement is also the peaceful preserve of diplomats and Paris's grande bourgeoisie.

Start: Ⓜ Ecole Militaire   **Finish:** Ⓜ Invalides

LOUVRE AND PALAIS-ROYAL

The Louvre, once a royal palace, is the city's most prized possession. Enclosed by three splendid wings, its famous glass pyramid reconciles past and future. Walk past the little triumphal arch of the Carrousel and cross over into the Tuileries gardens, adorned with sculptures by Maillol. You can return by the dazzling shopping street, Faubourg Saint-Honoré and the splendid Place Vendôme, where every other window displays the designs of famous jewellers or fashion houses. Spend some time in the sheltered gardens of the Palais-Royal.

THE DISTRICT AT A GLANCE

SIGHTS

Architecture
Place Vendôme 52
Galerie Vivienne.......54
Basilique Notre-Dame des Victoires 54
Galerie Véro-Dodat ★...........54
Eglise Saint-Germain-l'Auxerrois............54

Atmosphere
Rue de Rivoli 52
Palais-Royal ★..........53

Browsing
Le Louvre des Antiquaires..............53

Museums
Musée national du Louvre ★ 50
Musée des Arts décoratifs 51
Musée de la Publicité 51

Musée de la Mode et du Textile............51
Musée de l'Orangerie 52
Jeu de Paume (site Concorde) 52

Greenery
Jardin des Tuileries ...52

WALKING TOUR 56

WINING AND DINING 104

Musée national du Louvre (E3) If you want to enjoy the Louvre in relative peace, try to visit in the morning. Make sure you have plenty of time in hand, for the museum is far bigger than you imagine. And decide your priorities first: if you just wander aimlessly around, your brain will soon suffer from overload. Even a "highlights only" tour involves a great deal of walking. When the "new

Louvre" was opened in 1993, incorporating the three floors of the Richelieu Wing, the exhibition space doubled, making this the biggest museum in the world. Seven more rooms were added at the end of 1999 to display objets d'art from the first half of the 19th century. The main entrance is beneath I.M. Pei's glass pyramid in the middle of the Cour Napoléon, but you can also enter from the rue de Rivoli, opposite the Place du Palais Royal. Pick up a floor plan at the information desk to help you find your way around the labyrinth. The seven collections are grouped as follows: Greek, Etruscan and Roman Antiquities; Egyptian Antiquities (expanded to 5,000 objects in December 1997); Islamic Art; Oriental Antiquities; Applied Arts; paintings of the French, Italian, Spanish, Dutch, Flemish, German and English schools; and finally sculpture—superbly displayed in the three glassed-over courtyards of the Richelieu Wing. Beneath it all are the excavated ancient city walls and the **Carrousel du Louvre** designed by Jean-Michel Wilmotte, a gallery of 50 smart boutiques, post office, cash distributor, together with several fast-food restaurants and, near the Hall Napoléon, the CyberLouvre where you can surf through the museum's web site.
• Daily (except Tues and certain public holidays) 9am–6pm (Wed and Fri late closing at 10pm) ☎ 01 40 20 50 50 • Cour Napoléon (1st) Ⓜ Palais Royal–Musée du Louvre, Louvre–Rivoli ♿

Musée des Arts décoratifs (E3) The collections include furniture and soft furnishings, objets d'art, graphic arts, toys, glassware, accessories and jewellery from medieval times to the present, organized by period and by theme. Temporary exhibitions are held. The museum is in a wing of the Louvre, with its own entrance. • Tues–Fri 11am–6pm, late closing Thurs until 9pm; Sat, Sun 10am–6pm ☎ 01 44 55 57 50 • 107, rue de Rivoli (1st) Ⓜ Palais Royal–Musée du Louvre ♿

Musée de la Publicité (E3) Refurbished by Jean Nouvel, the museum analyses all aspects of advertising all over the world. • **Address and opening hours same as Musée des Arts décoratifs.** ♿

Musée de la Mode et du Textile (E3) If you are interested in changing fashions, don't miss this museum presenting 86,000 costumes, textiles and accessories from the 14th century to the present, in both permanent and

temporary exhibition. Contemporary fashion designers are well represented.
• Address and opening hours same as Musée des Arts décoratifs. ♿

Jardin des Tuileries (E3) Le Nôtre, the king's gardener, designed the vast Tuileries gardens in 1649, and they have been completely restored. The famous female nude statues by Aristide Maillol (1861–1944) are fetchingly displayed among low hedges in the Jardin du Carrousel. At the Concorde end is an attractive bookshop dedicated to gardening. • Place de la Concorde (1st) Ⓜ Palais-Royal, Tuileries, Concorde ♿

Musée de l'Orangerie (D3) This small museum, completely renovated to let natural light flood in, houses the delightful Walter-Guillaume collection of Impressionists: Cézanne, Renoir, Le Douanier Rousseau, Utrillo, Picasso and others. But the highlights are Monet's beautiful water-lily murals, *Les Nymphéas*, in their two oval rooms. • **Daily (except Tues) 9am–6pm for individual visitors only; groups must reserve. Closed May 1 and Dec 25** ☎ 01 44 77 80 07 • Jardin des Tuileries (1st) Ⓜ Concorde Ⓡ Invalides ♿

Jeu de Paume (site Concorde) (E3) The Orangerie's twin, on the rue de Rivoli side, is used for temporary exhibitions, films and conferences on photography and image (19th century to present day). • **Tues noon–9pm, Wed–Fri noon–7pm, Sat, Sun 10am–7pm** ☎ 01 47 03 12 50 • Jardin des Tuileries (1st) Ⓜ Concorde Ⓡ Invalides ♿

Rue de Rivoli (G4–E3) It stretches for what seems miles and miles, from Saint-Paul in the 4th arrondissement to the Place de la Concorde. The most interesting part is lined with arcades, opposite the Louvre and Tuileries, where you can escape from the noise of the traffic. Amid the souvenir shops, discount perfumeries, luxury hotels and bureaux de change, stop for a wicked hot chocolate at Angélina, an ultra-chic tearoom at no. 226. If you need an English magazine or paperback, call in at W.H. Smith, no. 248, at the Concorde end. It's worth going upstairs to see the carved friezes.

Place Vendôme (E3) The octagonal square is a prestigious address for most of the capital's jewellers—Van Cleef & Arpels, Chaumet, Boucheron. Napoleon

The fountains of Place de la Concorde were modelled on those of St Peter's Square, Rome, while the obelisk was sent from Luxor in a specially built ship.

Bonaparte, dressed as Caesar, watches all the action from his perch on the central column. • Ⓜ Opéra, Tuileries

Le Louvre des Antiquaires (E3) 250 up-market antique dealers, restaurant and delivery service. • Daily (except Tues) 11am–7pm. Closed Sun in July and August • 2, place du Palais-Royal (1st) Ⓜ Palais-Royal

Palais-Royal (E3) The Ministry of Culture and State Council have their quarters in the buildings overlooking a peaceful garden, only seconds away from the traffic. The secluded retreat, with rosebeds, fountains, sandpit and avenues of lime trees, is surrounded by arcades. The shops selling antiques, old books and prints, tin soldiers and wooden toys are utterly genteel, a far cry from 18th-century days when the Palais-Royal was riddled with gambling dens. Buren's black and white striped columns (1986) in the first courtyard are a favourite with children. • **Place du Palais-Royal (1st)** Ⓜ Palais-Royal

Galerie Vivienne (E3) Behind the gardens of the Palais Royal, this L-shaped covered arcade, linked with the Galerie Colbert, was declared a national historic monument in 1974. Its quiet corridors and vaulted, sculpted ceiling makie an eccentric setting for the startling designs of fashion whizz-kid Jean-Paul Gaultier (the windows of his boutique give onto rue Vivienne). At the other end of the arcade, the Brasserie is frequented by brokers from the nearby stock exchange. • **Starts 4, rue des Petits-Champs, ends 6, rue Vivienne (2nd)** Ⓜ Bourse

Basilique Notre-Dame des Victoires (F3) Rue Vide-Gousset, on the north side of elegant place des Victoires (where Thierry Mugler, Cacharel and Kenzo are based), leads to the basilica of Notre-Dame des Victoires, built to commemorate the royal victory over the protestants of La Rochelle in 1628. It was part of a convent that has now disappeared, and remains an important pilgrimage site. • **Place des Petits-Pères (2nd)** Ⓜ Bourse, Sentier

Galerie Véro-Dodat (F3) Named after the two pork butchers who founded it in 1824, this chic shopping arcade has mahogany shop-fronts, painted ceilings and a black and white tiled floor. • **Starts 19, rue J.-J. Rousseau, ends 2, rue du Bouloi (1st)** Ⓜ Louvre–Rivoli

Eglise Saint-Germain-l'Auxerrois (F3–4) Founded in Merovingian times, this Gothic church was expanded and remodelled several times before becoming the parish church of the kings of France, after the Louvre was built. Numerous artists who had found favour at court were buried there. A less glorious episode in its history: the bells of Saint-Germain tolled to announce the St Bartholomew's Day massacre. A short walk from here, in front of the protestant temple of the Oratoire (1, rue de l'Oratoire), stands a monument to the memory of the Huguenot leader Coligny, one of the famous victims of the massacre. • **Mon–Sat 8am–7 pm (Wed to 8.30pm), Sun 9am–8pm** • **2, place du Louvre (1st)** Ⓜ Louvre–Rivoli, Pont Neuf

GOING FOR A SONG

Every arrondissement has at least one food market, open two or three days a week (never on a Monday), from 7am to 1pm. Here is a small selection, in addition to the more specialized markets where you can rummage among old clothes, buy a canary or fall for an antique.

The **Marché du Temple**, rues Eugène-Spuller, Dupetit-Thouars and Perrée (3rd), Ⓜ Temple, combines boutiques and stalls filled with racks and heaps of clothes. Tues–Fri 9am–noon (boutiques until 7pm), Sat, Sun 9am–1pm.

Bargain-hunters are well acquainted with Place d'Aligre and Rue d'Aligre (12th), and their **Marché Beauvau Saint-Antoine**, Ⓜ Ledru-Rollin, held daily except Sun and Mon 7.30am–1pm. It sells food, jumble and second-hand clothes.

Antiquarian and second-hand books are sold at the **Marché du Livre ancien et d'occasion**, in a cast-iron building salvaged from the old Halles central market, Parc Georges-Brassens, rue Brancion (15th), Ⓜ Porte de Vanves, Sat, Sun 9am–6pm. With time and patience you may find a treasure, but you can also buy books by the kilo to fill up your shelves.

Customers fight over the cheap fabrics heaped up in the **Marché Saint-Pierre**, 2 rue Charles-Nodier (18th), Ⓜ Anvers. It offers the best selection in the capital, but you have to be quick.

There are two excellent **organic food markets**: boulevard Raspail (6th), Sun 9am–2pm Ⓜ Rennes, and boulevard des Batignolles (8th), Sat 9am–2pm Ⓜ Rome, Place de Clichy.

WALKING TOUR: BEHIND THE RUE DE RIVOLI

Head right on the arcaded **Rue de Rivoli**, where at no. 206, Tolstoy stayed in 1857 and, as he wrote, conceived a lifelong contempt for the bourgeoisie, to **Place des Pyramides**. The square has nothing to do with the Louvre's Pyramid nearby, but those of ancient Egypt, backdrop to a Napoleon victory in 1798. Its gilded 19th-century equestrian statue of another national hero, **Jeanne d'Arc**, is where France's extreme right wing rallies supporters for their parades.

North of the square across Rue Saint-Honoré, the 17th-century **Eglise Saint-Roch** is one of the city's biggest churches, its nave second in length only to Notre-Dame's, and fashionable burial place for such luminaries as playwright Corneille and philosopher Diderot. On **Rue Saint-Roch**, little old shops and a bistro (nos. 18, 20, 22) still use the church as their rear wall as in centuries past.

Turn left on Rue Gomboust to **Place du Marché Saint-Honoré** (1997), post-modernist Spanish architect Ricardo Bofill's characteristically gigantic glass temple to luxury consumerism—Italian furniture emporiums and showrooms for German cars.

On **Rue Saint-Honoré**, no. 211, the rear entrance of a hotel flanked by ornate store-fronts for a *pharmacie* and an underwear boutique was originally a façade of the great **Hôtel de Noailles** (1687). General La Fayette was married in its chapel in 1774, three years before he went off to fight for the American Revolution. Among the street's fashionable boutiques are the ultra-trendy Colette's at no. 213 and British fashion master John Galliano (no. 384). Opposite, adding a more sober note, is the Polish parish church, **Eglise de l'Assomption** (1676), with a bronze bust of native son John-Paul II at the entrance. Even more sobering is no. 398, last home of Robespierre before he was taken to the guillotine in 1794. Cheer the kids up (and your credit card company) at no. 406, where **Au Nain Bleu** is the oldest and quite the most luxurious toy shop in the city.

Turn left on **Rue Saint-Florentin** down to the US Consulate (no. 2, corner of Place de la Concorde), housed in a mansion where arch-Machiavellian diplomat Talleyrand died in 1838. The Americans bought it from the Rothschilds in 1950.

LOUVRE AND PALAIS-ROYAL

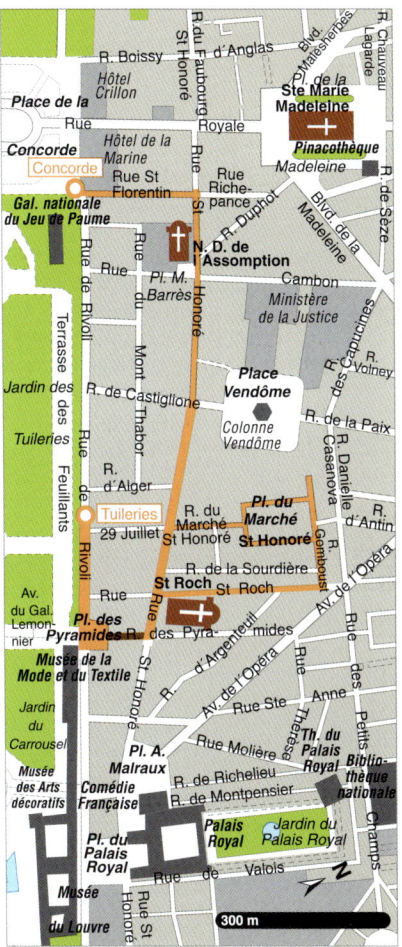

The back streets behind the arcades of the Rue de Rivoli offer a slice of French – and American – history and boutiques galore.

Start:
Ⓜ Tuileries

Finish:
Ⓜ Concorde

HALLES, MARAIS

This part of Paris has become quite trendy. In the 12th century the Knights Templar had the marshland on the right bank drained, and in 1605 Henri IV built the Royal Square, now Place des Vosges. Many members of the aristocracy were drawn to the district, constructing impressive mansions which you can still see today in the sector within rues Beaubourg and Turbigo, boulevard Beaumarchais, and rues de Rivoli and Saint-Antoine. When Louis XIV removed his court to Versailles, the district declined. Traders and artisans set up shop there, joined at the beginning of the 20th century by a number of Ashkenazy Jews. With its antique shops, galleries, tea rooms and gay bars, the Marais tends to get very crowded at weekends. The Halles was originally the central food market, transformed by the creation of the Pompidou Centre and the nearby Forum des Halles. Follow Rue des Francs-Bourgeois to Place des Vosges, then venture into the Jewish quarter around Rue des Rosiers, full of kosher and oriental grocery shops.

THE DISTRICT AT A GLANCE

SIGHTS

Architecture
Eglise St-Eustache....59
Tour Jean Sans Peur .59
Eglise St-Merri 60
Tour Saint-Jacques ...60
Hôtel de Ville 60
Cloître des Billettes ..60
Eglise St-Gervais-St-Protais 61
Place des Vosges ★...62
Hôtel de Sens 63

Atmosphere
Place Igor-Stravinsky.........60
Rue des Rosiers ★.....61

Browsing
Forum des Halles 59
BHV 60
Village Saint-Paul ★..63

Museums
Centre Pompidou.....59
Musée Picasso 61
Musée Cognacq-Jay .61
Musée Carnavalet....61
Maison de Victor Hugo 62
Jeu de Paume (site Sully).................62
Maison européenne de la Photographie 62
Mémorial de la Shoah 63

WALKING TOUR 64

WINING AND DINING 105

HALLES, MARAIS 59

Eglise Saint-Eustache (F3) Richelieu and Molière were baptised in this beautiful Flamboyant Gothic church. The stained-glass windows, dating from the 17th century, were crafted according to medieval traditions. Liszt and Berlioz played the organ in Saint-Eustache; free recitals are held on Sunday afternoons. • Mon–Fri 9.30am–7pm, Sat 10am–7pm, Sun 9am–7pm• 2, rue du Jour (1st) Ⓜ Les Halles ♿

Forum des Halles (F3) A vast subterranean shopping centre built around a glass and concrete patio, and due for extensive renovation starting in 2010. The Pavillon des Arts, one of the city museums, is an oasis of culture among all the commerce: it presents temporary exhibitions of all forms of art. • 1–7, rue Pierre-Lescot (1st) Ⓜ Les Halles ♿

Tour Jean Sans Peur (F3) You can climb to the top of this high medieval tower; the vault over the staircase is fantastically sculpted with leaves and flowers in the Flamboyant style. Temporary exhibitions and conferences. • Wed–Sun 1.30pm–6pm. Guided tours at 3pm ☎ 01 40 26 20 28 • 20, rue Etienne Marcel (4th) Ⓜ Etienne Marcel, Les Halles.

Centre national d'Art et de Culture Georges Pompidou (F3) Generally just called the Centre Pompidou, this project of the late 70s, by Richard Rogers and Renzo Piano, considered very daring at the time, has grown into its surroundings. Millions of visitors come here, some to wonder at the unseemly building with all its appendages of tubes, wires, shafts and air ducts, others to watch the street entertainment on the plaza, but the majority for the spectacular art exhibitions. The façade and interior have been extensively renovated, the cultural areas redesigned by Renzo Piano. The Museum of Modern Art on the 4th and 5th floors displays 25,000 works of the Fauvist, Cubist, Abstract, Dadaist and Surrealist schools. The building also houses a public library and centre for musical research. Paying visitors to the museum can take the external escalator to watch the view of Paris unfurling through the windows (best seen from the 4th floor). Panoramic restaurant on the 6th floor. Good art bookshop with a great selection of postcards. • **Daily (except Tues and May 1) 11am–9pm. Library daily 11am–10pm** ☎ 01 44 78 12 33 • Plateau Beaubourg (4th) Ⓜ Rambuteau ⓇⒺⓇ Châtelet-Les Halles ♿

Place Igor-Stravinsky (F3) Just round the corner from the Pompidou Centre, a pleasant square where you can sit and contemplate the colourful mobiles by Jean Tingueley and his wife Niki de Saint-Phalle in the fountain. Ⓜ Hôtel de Ville

Eglise Saint-Merri (F3–4) This Flamboyant Gothic church was built during the Renaissance, and the interior was "baroquified" in the 18th century. Undergoing restoration. • **Daily 9am–7pm** • **78, rue Saint-Martin or 76, rue de la Verrerie (4th)** Ⓜ Hôtel de Ville

Tour Saint-Jacques (F4) This Flamboyant Gothic tower is all that remains of the Church Saint-Jacques-de-la-Boucherie, a departure point for pilgrims bound for Santiago de Compostella. It has been restored to its former splendour. Unfortunately you cannot visit the interior. • **Square de la Tour Saint-Jacques** Ⓜ Hôtel de Ville.

Hôtel de Ville (F4) The Town Hall was rebuilt in neo-Renaissance style just three years after supporters of the Commune sent the old one up in flames. The façade's 136 statues represent French citizens (the males) and French towns (the females). Temporary history and art exhibitions are organized here, and there are free tours of the magnificent salons. • **Individual visitors and groups Mon–Fri by appointment** ☎ **01 42 76 50 49** • **Place de l'Hôtel de Ville (4th)** Ⓜ Hôtel de Ville ♿

Bazar de l'Hôtel de Ville (F4) Irresistible selection of doorknobs, brass keyholes, curtain rings and fabrics in the home furnishings department, but the BHV basement is a do-it-yourself paradise. From the self-service restaurant you get a good view of Saint-Gervais church and the Town Hall. • **Mon, Tues, Thurs, Fri, Sat 9.30am–7.30pm, Wed 9.30am–9pm** • **52–64, rue de Rivoli (4th)** Ⓜ Hôtel de Ville

Cloître des Billettes (F4) Dating from 1427, this is the only surviving medieval cloister in Paris. It was built on the ruins of the house of a Jewish merchant accused of having stabbed and burned a Host. Its Flamboyant Gothic vaults make a superb setting for concerts and exhibitions. The adjoining church has been used for Protestant worship since 1812. • **22–26, rue des Archives (4th)** Ⓜ Hôtel de Ville

Eglise Saint-Gervais-Saint-Protais (F–G4) The church was built on the site of a Merovingian shrine dedicated to the brothers Gervais and Protais, both martyrs. Dating from the 17th century, the church combines a Gothic nave with a classic façade. While you're in the neighbourhood, pop into the shop opposite the church (10, rue des Barres) selling produce of the monastical communities: jam, honey, biscuits, elixirs and potions. • **Daily 6am–9pm** • **Place Saint-Gervais (4th)** Ⓜ Hôtel de Ville

Musée Picasso (G3) The Hôtel Salé, a large 17th-century townhouse, makes a handsome setting for Picasso's personal collection of ceramics and paintings: works by Matisse, Cézanne, Miró and Renoir, with his own paintings, sculpture, photographs and documents. The museum furniture was designed by the Swiss sculptor Diego Giacometti; it was his last commission, accomplished at the age of 80. • **Daily (except Tues), summer 9.30am–6pm, winter 9.30am–5.30pm** ☏ **01 42 71 25 21** • **Hôtel Salé, 5, rue de Thorigny (3rd)** Ⓜ St-Paul ♿

Musée Cognacq-Jay (G4) Ernest Cognacq and Louise Jay founded the department store La Samaritaine. They bequeathed their huge collection of 18th-century paintings to the city of Paris: delicate works by Fragonard, Chardin and Boucher, now displayed here in the Hôtel Donon. • **Daily (except Mon) 10am–6pm. Free admission** • **8, rue Elzévir (3rd)** Ⓜ St-Paul

Musée Carnavalet (G4) The 16th-century town house of compulsive epistle-writer Mme de Sévigné was converted into a museum in 1880, tracing the history of Paris up to the reign of Louis XVI. The neighbouring mansion, Hôtel Le Peletier de Saint-Fargeau, houses the collections covering the period from the Revolution to modern times. Pleasant, quiet garden. • **Daily (except Mon and public holidays) 10am–6pm. Free admission** • **23, rue de Sévigné (3rd)** Ⓜ St-Paul, Chemin Vert

Rue des Rosiers (G4) This is the heart of the Jewish quarter. Goldenberg's restaurant and takeaway at no. 7 are renowned. Sacha Finkelsztajn, a yellow-fronted deli at no. 27, sells Central European and Russian specialities, as does Florence Finkelsztajn in the blue shop on the corner with rue des Ecouffes. You may well have to queue, but it's worth a wait for a slice of poppy-seed strudel. Ⓜ St Paul

Place des Vosges (G4) This square is a study in harmony and symmetry, featuring 36 red-brick houses, four centuries old, around a formal garden laid out with gravel paths and fountains. It was built on the site of a textile manufacture by Henri IV, who employed the best architects, painters and sculptors. People are now allowed to sit on the grass, and things get very lively on summer afternoons. In the centre is an equestrian statue of Louis XIII, set up by Richelieu in 1639. Peep into the double courtyard of no. 9 for a glimpse into the past. Ⓜ Chemin Vert, Bastille ♿

Maison de Victor Hugo (G4) Victor Hugo lived in this cosy seven-room apartment from 1833 to 1848. He wrote a few chapters of *Les Misérables* here, and made some of the furniture. More than 400 of his drawings, plus letters and manuscripts, are on display. Regular exhibitions. • Daily (except Mon and public holidays) 10am–6pm. Free admission • Hôtel de Rohan-Guéménée, 6, place des Vosges (4th) Ⓜ Chemin Vert, Bastille

Jeu de Paume (site Sully) (G4) Exhibitions devoted to the relationship between photography and advertising, housed in the Hôtel de Sully. Built in 1624 by Maximilien de Béthune, Grand Master of the Artillery of the Arsenal, the superb Renaissance mansion is also the headquarters of the national register of Historical Monuments (Monum) and the national heritage library. You can reach it through the garden via a charming passage at 7, place des Vosges. • Tues– Fri noon–7pm, Sat, Sun 10am–7pm • Hôtel de Sully, 62, rue Saint-Antoine (4th) Ⓜ St-Paul, Bastille ♿

Maison européenne de la Photographie (G4) In an 18th-century mansion, a permanent collection of more than 15,000 photographs from the 1950s to the present day, with a room devoted to Irving Penn. Also workshops, vidéothèque and library, and a café in vaulted rooms. • Daily (except Mon, Tues and public holidays) 11am–8pm • 5–7, rue de Fourcy (4th) Ⓜ St-Paul

Sunlight illuminates the Forum des Halles, an underground shopping mall.

Mémorial de la Shoah (G4) Sober, beautifully designed, permanent exhibition and reading-room devoted to the fate of Europe's Jews in World War II, with special emphasis on individual cases during the deportation from France during the German Occupation. • **Daily (except Sat) 10am–6pm, Thurs 10am–10pm** • 17 rue Geoffroy-l'Asnier (4th) Ⓜ Saint Paul

Hôtel de Sens (G4) A rare vestige of medieval Paris, this splendid turreted mansion was built between 1475 and 1519 for the archbishop of Sens, at the time when Paris was a mere bishopric dependent on the Burgundy city. Henri IV's queen Margot lived there for several years. • **Bibliothèque Forney: Tues, Fri, Sat 1–7.30pm; Wed, Thurs 10am–7.30pm** • 1, rue du Figuier (4th) Ⓜ Pont Marie

Village Saint-Paul (G4) An intricate maze of streets where every other shop sells enticing antiques. • **Thurs–Mon 11am–7pm** • Between the quai des Célestins, Rue Saint-Paul and Rue Charlemagne (4th) Ⓜ St-Paul

WALKING TOUR: HALLES – MARAIS

The Métro's Rue Rambuteau exit leads to the splendid church of **Saint-Eustache** (1532–1644). To take in the Flamboyant Gothic exterior as far as its startling neoclassical western façade, cross the sloping forecourt between roller-bladers and skateboarders whizzing around a giant head-and-hand sculpture. Follow signs to the **Jardin de Fleurs** over a footbridge between glass pyramids of exotic flowers and turn left past the great domed **Bourse du Commerce** (Commodities Exchange, Corn Market in the 18th century). Walk back to the **Forum des Halles** on Allée Blaise Cendrars past *boules* players under the plane trees.

Back on Rue Rambuteau, cross Boulevard Sébastopol to the **Centre Pompidou**. If you're not catching the escalator view of Paris rooftops or being caricatured by a street-artist, head to Place Igor-Stravinsky and the jolly **Fontaine Stravinsky**. Watch its mechanical sculptures twirling in the water and have a *crêpe* at one of the poolside cafés.

Past the church of **Saint-Merri**, another Flamboyant Gothic gem, cut behind the Centre Pompidou to cross Rue du Renard. At no. 12, notice the handsome Art nouveau façade of the **Syndicat de l'épicerie française** (French Grocers' Guild, 1902) with its Three Musketeers' slogan *Tous pour un, un pour tous* (All for one, one for all). Rue Saint-Merri turns off into the **Marais** proper. The Gai Moulin is just one of many places on and around **Rue Sainte-Croix de la Bretonnerie** announcing—in all senses of the word—the gay colours of the quarter's new restaurants, cafés, boutiques and art galleries. From Rue Vieille du Temple, turn right into **Rue des Rosiers**, heart of the old Jewish quarter recently beautified by trees and flower beds. Along with Hebrew bookshops are bakeries and delicatessens of Ashkenazi Jews from Central Europe and falafel bars and chic boutiques of Sephardic Jews from southern Europe and North Africa. The old Hammam steam bath at no. 4 is now a smart furniture shop. At the far end, no. 3 is a very cosy British-style tea room, Le Loir dans la Théière (Dormouse in the Teapot). Rue Pavée brings you to **Rue des Francs-Bourgeois**, the main thoroughfare of the Marais lined with its most trendy shops. To the right is Henri IV's **Place des Vosges**, one of Europe's most elegant squares and grand "terminus" for the walk.

HALLES, MARAIS

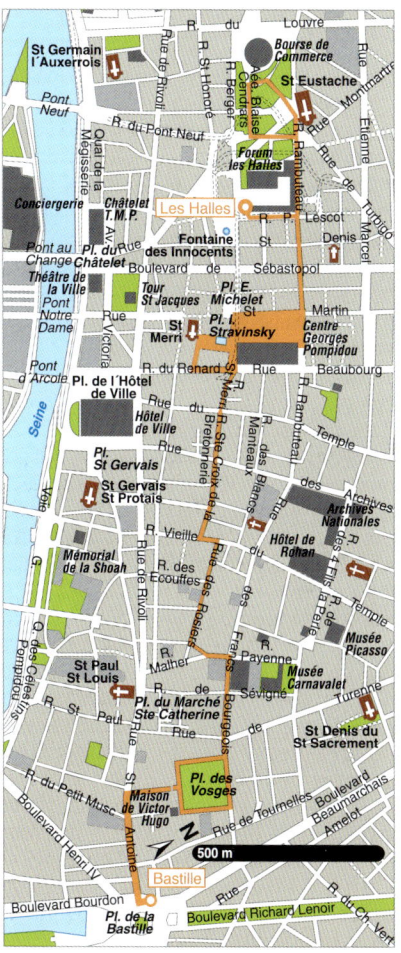

Once the "belly" of Paris, Les Halles' old market district is now a bustling shopping and garden area next to the Marais, a long-established Jewish neighbourhood shared these days with a lively new gay community.

Start:
Ⓜ Les Halles

Finish:
Ⓜ Bastille

BASTILLE, BERCY, BELLEVILLE

Place de la Bastille, dominated by the gleaming white Opéra of pharaonic proportions, is at the heart of the clubbers' district, between boulevards Richard Lenoir, Voltaire and rue du Faubourg Saint-Antoine. North of the Gare du Lyon, up to rue Crozatier, hundreds of computer technology specialists have set up shop around the "computer cybermarket" Surcouf. Along the Seine, past the Palais Omnisport and the Parc de Bercy, is the new Village de Bercy. From there, you can cross the river by the Pont de Tolbiac to reach the Bibliothèque de France. North of the Père-Lachaise cemetery, Belleville is getting ever more trendy, while the site of the old abattoirs has been given a new lease of life as the City of Sciences and Industry.

THE DISTRICT AT A GLANCE

SIGHTS

Atmosphere
Place de la Bastille ...66

Faubourg Saint-Antoine ...68

Cinémathèque française ...68

Cimetière du Père-Lachaise ★ ...69

Browsing
Marché Bastille ...67

Viaduc des Arts ★ ...68

Bercy Village ...68

Museums
Musée des Arts forains ...68

Cité des Sciences et de l'Industrie ★ ...68

Musée de la Musique ...69

Greenery
Canal Saint-Martin ...67

Parc de Belleville ...69

WALKING TOUR 70

WINING AND DINING 107

Place de la Bastille (G4) Symbol of the absolute monarchy, the infamous Bastille fortress was one of eleven guarding the capital, known and feared mostly as a prison: Fouquet, the Man in the Iron Mask, Voltaire, the Marquis de Sade were all locked up there at one time or another. But there were only six prisoners in the cells when, on July 14th, 1789, the people of Paris stormed

A bucolic atmosphere along the banks of the Canal Saint-Martin.

the Bastille. Today there is no trace of the past. The column in the middle of the square was erected to honour the victims of the 1830 Revolution. To the south is the Opéra-Bastille, and the boating harbour (Port de Plaisance de l'Arsenal) on the Saint-Martin canal, which passes underground beneath the square and Boulevard Richard-Lenoir, emerging into daylight further north at rue du Faubourg du Temple. Cruises start at the harbour. Ⓜ Bastille

Marché Bastille (G4) Everything from live crabs to sewing machines is sold in this cheerful street market beneath the trees and above the Canal Saint-Martin. • **Food: Thurs, Sun 7am–1.30pm. Flea market: Sat dawn to dusk** • Bd Richard-Lenoir (11th) Ⓜ Bastille, Bréguet-Sabin

Canal Saint-Martin (G3–2) The tree-lined banks are a favourite walk of Parisian families who delight in the locks and romantic footbridges. There are several possibilities for canal cruises. • **Between Square Jules-Ferry and Boulevard de La Villette (10th)** Ⓜ République, Jacques Bonsergent, Jaurès

Faubourg Saint-Antoine (H4) In the 15th century, the artisans living on the lands of the abbey of Saint-Antoine-des-Champs were granted freedom from the supervision of the corporations, and from that time onwards, the district was colonized by carpenters and cabinetmakers. The tradition endures, but since the 1980s, architects (Wilmotte), fashion designers (Gaultier) and all kinds of artists have infused the faubourg with a new lease of life. Parallel Rue de Lappe, once the place to tango, is lined with trendy cafés and discothèques. Ⓜ Bastille, Ledru-Rollin, Faidherbe-Chaligny

Viaduc des Arts (H5) The old redbrick railway viaduct running along Avenue Daumesnil has been beautifully restored, and the arches have been rehabilitated as workshops for artisans and designers. You can windowshop all the way down, and walk or jog back again along the top, transformed into a shrub-lined walkway called the "promenade plantée". Ⓜ Gare de Lyon

Bercy Village (H5) A number of identical stone wine warehouses around a paved courtyard, all carefully restored to house boutiques, leisure facilities, bars and restaurants, along with the Club Med adventure and travel centre and a multi-screen cinema. The village is very popular with Parisians on Sundays. • Daily 11am–9pm (the restaurants close at 2am) Ⓜ Cour St-Emilion ♿

Musée des Arts forains (H6) A splendid collection of merry-go-rounds, shooting galleries: all the fun of the fair from 1850 to the present. Groups (min. 15) only. ☎ 01 43 40 16 22 • Pavillons de Bercy, 53, av. des Terroirs de France (12th) Ⓜ Cour St-Emilion ♿

Cinémathèque française (H6) The French cinémathèque is housed in the American Center, designed by Frank Gehry. Apart from showing films, it organizes exhibitions, workshops and discussions. The Bibliothèque du Film (BIFI) documents the history of the cinema. • **Exhibitions Mon, Wed, Fri, Sat noon–7pm, Thurs noon–10pm, Sun 10am–8pm; library Mon, Wed–Fri 10am–7pm, Sat 1–6.30pm** ☎ 01 71 19 33 33 • 51, rue de Bercy (12th) Ⓜ Bercy

Cité des Sciences et de l'Industrie (H1) Even if the words "science" and "industry" make you shudder, you'll enjoy this vast hands-on activity centre which refuses to call itself a museum. The permanent exhibition covers four main themes—the universe, the earth, space and the environment—in such a way as to make it all genuinely fascinating for people of all ages. The Cinaxe is a "moving" movie theatre and the Argonaute a real hunter submarine. The gleaming silver spherical Géode, by far the biggest draw, has a hemispheric screen showing films on nature, the environment and discovery. • **Cité des Sciences: daily (except Mon and public holidays) 10am–6pm, Sun 10am–7pm** ☏ 01 40 05 70 00. Géode: Tues–Sun 10.30am–9.30pm; a film is shown every hour. ☏ 01 40 05 79 99 • 30, av. Corentin-Cariou (19th) Ⓜ Porte de la Villette

Musée de la Musique (H1) Permanent and temporary exhibitions representing music from around the world. The collections comprise more than 900 instruments, paintings, sculpture and various objects with musical connections. Concerts are held at the Cité de la Musique. Information www.cite-musique.fr • **Tues–Sat noon–6pm, Sun 10am–6pm** ☏ 01 44 84 44 84 • Cité de la Musique, 221, avenue Jean-Jaurès (19th) Ⓜ Porte de Pantin ♿

Cimetière du Père-Lachaise (H3–4) Since Jim Morrison, of the *Doors*, was buried here in 1971, this has become the most visited cemetery in the world. All day long, streams of teenage admirers come to light a candle or lay a memento on his tomb, leaving a trail of graffiti in their wake. A million people are buried in Père-Lachaise and it is something of a labyrinth; the best way to find the tombs of the famous—Chopin, Delacroix, Oscar Wilde, Simone Signoret, Edith Piaf, Michel Petrucciani and too many more—is to buy a map at the entrance. • **Daily, summer 8am–6pm, winter 8am–5.30 pm** • 16, rue du Repos (20th) Ⓜ Philippe Auguste

Parc de Belleville (H1) You'll get a superb view of Paris from the heights of this park in the Belleville district. It descends in terraces, past rocks and vineyards, enlivened by waterfalls and fountains. There are several playgrounds, and the Maison de l'Air, a museum that will entertain anyone interested in meteorology. • **Maison de l'Air: daily (except Mon) March–Oct 1.30–5.30pm; Nov–Feb 1.30–5pm** ☏ 01 43 28 47 63 • 27, rue Piat (20th) Ⓜ Belleville

WALKING TOUR: AROUND THE BASTILLE

As a reminder of July 14, 1789, start out on the métro **Bastille platform of Line 1** (La Défense-Vincennes) where colourful ceramic panels depict the seizure of the prison and its aftermath. Exit Rue de Lyon for a rear view of the Opéra-Bastille and turn left on Avenue Daumesnil. The avenue's 19th-century railway viaduct has been handsomely redesigned by Patrick Berger and Jean-Michel Wilmotte as the **Viaduc des Arts**—50 galleries and ateliers installed in redbrick archways to showcase furniture, textiles, glassware, ceramics, leatherware and other arts and crafts. Overhead (stairs at Avenue Ledru-Rollin and Rue Hector Malot) the viaduct has been landscaped with trees, shrubs and flowers to create a pretty **Promenade Plantée** all the way along the avenue.

Beneath the viaduct, take Rue Hector Malot, left on Rue Charenton and then right on Rue d'Aligre to the **Marché d'Aligre**, where one of Paris's liveliest open-air markets (mornings only) shares the square with the covered Marché Beauvau (also afternoons from 4pm). From the far left of the square, Rue Théophile Roussel leads to **Square Trousseau**, its trendy restaurant and a children's playground with a nice soft cork-like surface to fall over on, and an old-fashioned bandstand.

Right on Rue du Faubourg Saint-Antoine, left on Rue Trousseau and right on Rue de Candie to Massimiliano Fuksas' eye-catching low-cost modern sports and apartment complex, **Ilot Candie-Saint-Bernard** (1996), with its undulating, sea-wave-like roof.

Return via Rue Charles Delescluze to Rue Trousseau and continue right to **Rue de Charonne**. At no. 53, set back behind a modern apartment building, is the elegant 17th-century **Hôtel de Mortagne**; you can admire its façade from the Passage Charles Dallery.

Back on Rue de Charonne, explore its picturesque *passages*, courtyards and side-streets—left down **Passage l'Homme** for its ivy-covered artists' studios; right on cobble-stoned **Rue de Lappe**, famous for its pre-war *bals-musette*, of which Le Balajo (no. 9) is a relic, and now teeming with more modern nightspots. Cross Rue La Roquette to Rue Daval and turn at no. 12 to the shops and galleries of **Cour Damoye**, leading back to the Bastille.

BASTILLE, BERCY, BELLEVILLE

Few stone relics remain from the birthplace of the French Republic, but the rejuvenated neighbourhood stays ever alive to change.

Start and Finish: Ⓜ Bastille

The Aligre market is closed Monday.

GRANDS BOULEVARDS

The name, big boulevards, refers to the straight, wide avenues that converge on the Opéra-Garnier, the business centre and entertainment district with its theatres, music halls and grand cafés: boulevard des Italiens, des Capucines, Haussmann and Montmartre. Big-time shoppers head for the department stores on Boulevard Haussmann, Au Printemps and Galeries Lafayette.

THE DISTRICT AT A GLANCE

SIGHTS	Atmosphere	Museums
Architecture	Boulevard Haussmann 72	Pinacothèque de Paris 73
Eglise de la Madeleine 72	Paris Story 74	Musée du Parfum.....73
Palais Garnier ★ 74	Passage du Caire 74	Musée Grévin 74
Société Générale......74	**Treats**	**WALKING TOUR** 76
	Gourmet foods ★......75	**WINING AND DINING** 107

Boulevard Haussmann (E2) At no. 40, **Galeries Lafayette** has preserved its 1910 façade and a superb stained-glass cupola. It specializes in perfumes, cosmetics, lingerie, kitchenware, furnishings, electric fittings and fashion. The food department is excellent. **Au Printemps**, at no. 64, is good for trendy young fashions. There's a big perfume department, and an excellent choice of kitchenware and stationery. The Art Nouveau stained-glass cupola over the "Espace Flo" café-restaurant is a listed monument. View of Montmartre from the 9th floor terrace. Ⓜ Havre-Caumartin

Eglise de la Madeleine (E2–D3) With its peristyle of Corinthian columns, the Madeleine church looks more like a displaced Parthenon. Its construction, begun for Louis XV in 1764, was halted by the Revolution. Napoleon dithered between a bank, a theatre and a library before deciding to turn the unfinished

Cherubs cavort on the façade of Garnier's Opéra, a temple to the musical arts.

building into a temple dedicated to his Grand Army. It was completed and consecrated as a Catholic church under Louis XVIII. • **Daily 7am–7pm** • **Place de la Madeleine (8th)** Ⓜ Madeleine Ⓡ Auber

Pinacothèque de Paris (E2) Formerly the Musée Baccarat, this building has been transformed into an immense art gallery, where temporary exhibitions from private collections are spread over three floors. • **Daily 10.30am–6pm. Ticket booth closes at 5.15pm** • **28, pl. de la Madeleine (8th)** Ⓜ Madeleine Ⓡ Auber

Musée du Parfum (E2) The Belle-Epoque Théâtre des Capucines houses a fascinating museum tracing the fragrant, 3,000-year history of perfume and cosmetics. A similar museum is located near the Opéra-Garnier at 9, rue Scribe. Both are run by the Fragonard company. • **Mon–Sat 9am–6pm. Free admission** • **39, bd des Capucines (2nd)** Ⓜ Opéra

Opéra National de Paris–Palais Garnier (E2) The theatre built for Napoleon III is now the seat of the National Ballet. Despite its imposing size, only 2,000 spectators fit into the circular space crowned by a ceiling painted by Chagall in 1964, with a sparkling 6-ton chandelier. At the boutique, you can buy musical souvenirs as well as pots of honey harvested from the hives on the building's roof. The opera library and museum, 8, rue Scribe, open 10am–5pm, displays interesting collections of drawings, paintings, stage sets and costumes.
• Tours daily 10am–5pm. The doors close at 4.30pm ☎ 08 92 89 90 90
• Place de l'Opéra (2nd) Ⓜ Opéra

Paris Story (E2) Three attractions: Paris-Story, an audiovisual show on a giant screen, taking you through 20 centuries of history in 50 minutes of poetry and music. Paris-Miniature: interactive relief map of Paris, on a scale of 1:5000, with 150 touch slides and monuments. Paris-Experience: video gallery showing five clips, and free Internet access to information about Paris. • Daily 10am–6pm, Paris-Story shows on every hour. ☎ 01 42 66 62 06 • 11bis, rue Scribe (9th) Ⓜ Opéra Ⓡ Auber

Société Générale (E2) The Paris headquarters of this large bank is an Art Nouveau masterpiece designed by architect Jacques Hermant, complete with stained-glass windows and panels. • Tours during bank opening hours • 29, bd Haussmann (9th) Ⓜ Opéra Ⓡ Auber

Grévin (F2) The famous wax museum founded in 1882 presents 300 characters straight out of history and the cinema. The entrance is in passage Jouffroy, a Belle Epoque covered arcade. • Mon–Fri 10am– 6.30pm, Sat, Sun and public holidays 10am–7pm. Last tickets one hour before closing ☎ 01 47 70 85 05 • 10, bd Montmartre (9th) Ⓜ Grands Boulevards ♿

Passage du Caire (F3) The Sentier district has long been synonymous with the rag trade, but now, because of the low rents and huge lofts, it has been taken over by telecommunications and Internet companies. There's still something of the souk in the "Cairo arcade", with its neo-Egyptian architecture, full of inexpensive clothes shops; it's the oldest shopping gallery in Paris.
• Starts 2, place du Caire, ends 33, rue d'Alexandrie (2nd) Ⓜ Sentier

FOOD, GLORIOUS FOOD

Place de la Madeleine has several gourmet temples. It is difficult to decide which is the more tempting, **Hédiard**, at no. 21, or **Fauchon**, no. 26, famed for its mouthwatering window displays. At the **Maison de la Truffe**, no. 19, you can drool over black and white truffles, foie gras, caviare, smoked salmon and other luxury goodies. Or why not sample some caviare in **Caviar Kaspia**, no. 17 (shop and restaurant). The **Nicolas** flagship wineshop at no. 31 concentrates on prestigious names. **La Maison du Chocolat** sells luscious home-made chocolates, marrons glacés, macaroons and other confectionary. The **Boutique Maille**, no. 6, specializes in countless varieties of Dijon mustard in pretty jars of all sizes, perfect for gifts – choose a pot and it will be filled from a pump. The **Verger de la Madeleine**, 4 bd Malesherbes, offers a great range of the best French wines. For crusty breads and irresistible pastries, head for the bakery and salon de thé **Paul** on Rue Royale. **Lafayette Gourmet**, 40, bd Haussmann, is the right bank's answer to the Bon Marché's Grande Epicerie (see p. 42).

WALKING TOUR: PALAIS-ROYAL AND THE GALLERIES

This walk takes you through the district south of Boulevard Montmartre. The Métro's Place Colette exit is a bizarre coloured-glass conglomeration, *Kiosque des noctambules* (Night-Owls' Pavilion), "honouring" Guimard's beloved Art nouveau designs for other stations. Past the Comédie Française in the Ministry of Culture's courtyard are Buren's once controversial, now popular black and white columns, leading to the **Palais-Royal**. Its gardens enjoy a secluded tranquillity—shady avenues of lime trees around cool fountains, green lawns with flowered borders and comfortable benches for reading or snoozing. In the 18th-century arcades, **Galerie de Montpensier** boutiques sell medals, rare stamps, wonderful tin soldiers (no. 14), antique and modern jewellery and second-hand high fashion, opposite more modern, but still classical shops, including very chic garden implements (no. 37) in **Galerie de Valois**.

From the gardens' southeast exit, cross Rue de Valois and take Rue du Colonel-Driant to the Rue du Bouloi entrance of **Galerie Véro-Dodat**. In 1826, two pork butchers made this black-and-white-paved arcade with shop-fronts of mahogany, bronze and brass a fashionable—and dry—short-cut between Les Halles and the Palais-Royal. Don't miss Robert Capa's lovely doll shop.

Doubling back to Rue du Bouloi, turn right on Rue Croix-des-Petits-Champs to the **Banque de France** and admire on Rue de La Vrillière its grand neoclassical portal by François Mansart. Carry on to Rue des Petits-Champs and the entrance at no. 4 to **Galerie Vivienne**, the most stylish of the city's shopping arcades. L-shaped to emerge on Rue Vivienne, it varies its mosaic-paved spaces in a lively mix of antiques, toys, old books, tea-rooms (most elegantly À Priori Thé) and wild fashions of Jean-Paul Gaultier. Next door, **Galerie Colbert** (6 Rue Vivienne) is more august, restored for the Institut National d'histoire de l'art, but enlivened by the 1920s décor of its brasserie.

If you have time for more passages and more boutiques, continue past the Bourse to Rue Saint Marc, cross over and turn right for the entrance to the Passage des Panoramas, which leads to Boulevard Montmartre, Passage Jouffroy and Passage Verdeau.

GRANDS BOULEVARDS 77

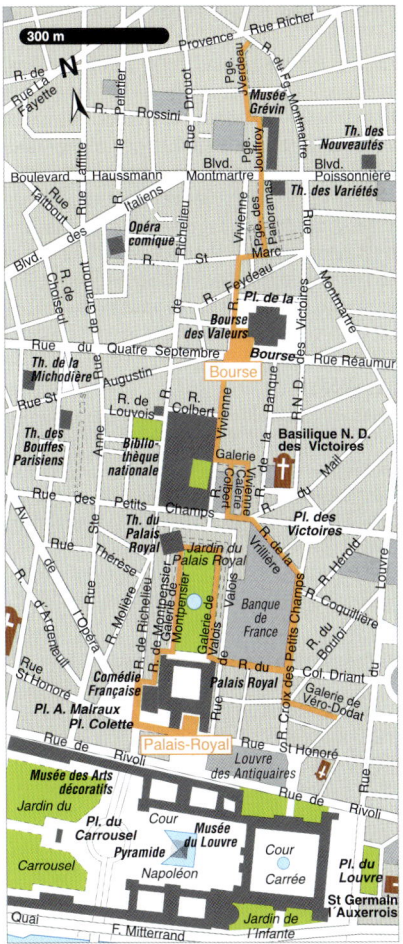

On a cosy scale, Paris's Galleries were a 19th-century precursor to the modern shopping mall. Four of them are close by the gardens of the Palais Royal, itself surrounded by its own venerable shopping arcades.

Start:
Ⓜ Palais Royal

Finish:
Ⓜ Bourse

CHAMPS-ÉLYSÉES AND THE WEST

The avenue des Champs-Elysées is busy day and night, with an endless stream of traffic. Strollers tramp up and down the wide pavements beneath the trees, passing, without even realising it, the gardens of the Elysée Palace, home of the French President. Halfway along at the Rond-Point (roundabout), you can turn into select Avenue Montaigne, where many of the big names in designer fashion have their quarters. Avenue Foch, the wide thoroughfare branching off from Place Charles-de-Gaulle, takes you into the residential 16th arrondissement, founded in 1860 by combining the communes of Chaillot, Auteuil and Passy and bounded by the Bois de Boulogne, the remains of a vast forest.

THE DISTRICT AT A GLANCE

SIGHTS

Architecture
Arc de Triomphe........80

Palais de Chaillot
et Esplanade
du Trocadéro............82

Grande Arche
de la Défense 85

Atmosphere
Place de
la Concorde............79

Avenue des
Champs-Elysées........79

Browsing
Marché aux Timbres..80

Musée Dapper..........80

Fashion designers 85

Museums
Petit Palais – Musée
des Beaux-Arts de la
Ville de Paris............79

Galeries nationales du
Grand Palais............79

Palais de
la Découverte..........80

Musée Cernuschi ★ ..80

Musée Nissim de
Camondo 81

Musée Jacquemart-
André ★....................80

Musée des Arts
asiatiques – Guimet..81

Musée Baccarat 81

Musée de la Mode de
la Ville de Paris 82

Musée d'Art
moderne de la
Ville de Paris............82

Palais de Tokyo 82

Muséum national
d'Histoire naturelle –
Musée de l'Homme..82

Cité de l'architecture
et du patrimoine 83

Musée national
de la Marine 83

Musée du Vin 84

Maison de Balzac......84

Musée Marmottan-
Monet......................84

CHAMPS-ÉLYSÉES AND THE WEST 79

Greenery	Jardin	**WALKING TOUR** 86
Parc Monceau..........80	d'Acclimatation 84	
Bois de Boulogne.....84	Parc de Bagatelle.....85	**WINING AND DINING** 108
Jardin Shakespeare ..84		

Place de la Concorde (D3) See it at night, when it's quieter and the fountains are illuminated. The granite obelisk from the temple of Ramses II in Louxor dates from 1300 BC. It was set up here in 1836, a gift from Mohammed Ali, viceroy of Egypt, and crowned by a golden "pyramidion" in May 1998. All the fountains and columns by Jacques Hittorff have been restored and refreshed with a new coat of dark green paint and gold trim. Ⓜ Concorde

Avenue des Champs-Elysées (D3) Like Trafalgar Square in London, this is where everyone gathers for important events. The avenue stretches along the great vista sweeping from the Louvre to the Arc de Triomphe, with the modern district of the Défense and its white marble arch just visible in the haze beyond. Both sides of the avenue are lined with cafés, cinemas and boutiques, all open on Sunday. Ⓜ Franklin D. Roosevelt

Petit Palais – Musée des Beaux-Arts de la Ville de Paris (D3) Built for the 1900 World's Fair, the gleaming glass structure, magnificently restored, houses the city's collection of Fine Arts, from Greek Antiquity to World War I. • Daily (except Mon and holidays) 10am–6pm; Thurs 10am–8 pm during temporary exhibitions • Av. Winston-Churchill (8th) Ⓜ Champs-Elysées-Clemenceau ♿

Galeries nationales du Grand Palais (D3) A Belle Epoque palace built for the 1900 World's Fair and to glorify French Art. It was transformed into exhibition halls in 1964 by André Malraux, when he was Minister of Culture. Newly restored, it is now used for temporary blockbuster exhibitions. See the two splendid quadrigas on the roof by Georges Récipon. • Hours vary according to exhibitons • Av. du Général-Eisenhower (8th) Ⓜ Champs-Elysées-Clemenceau

Palais de la Découverte (D3) In a wing of the Grand Palais, the "Palace of Discovery" strives to make science seem like fun. Children love the Planetarium, and in the Cybermétropole you can play on the computers and enjoy an hour's free access to Internet. • Daily (except Mon) 9.30am–6pm, Sun and public holidays 10am–7pm • Av. Franklin-Roosevelt (8th) Ⓜ Champs-Elysées-Clemenceau Ⓡ Invalides ♿

Marché aux Timbres (D3) The serious stamp-collector's favourite rendez-vous has expanded to include phonecards and other collectibles. • Thurs, Sat, Sun and public holidays 10am–6pm • Cours Marigny (8th) Ⓜ Champs-Elysées-Clemenceau

Musée Dapper (C2) This little-known museum is dedicated to providing an artistic and cultural space for Africa, the Caribbean and their diasporas. It holds permanent and temporary exhibitions, conferences and dance performances.
• Daily (except Tues) 11am–7pm • 35, rue Paul Valéry (16th) Ⓜ Victor Hugo

Parc Monceau (D2) The 19th-century version of an English park, dotted with romantic follies such as Greek-looking remains and neo-Gothic ruins. • 58, bd Courcelles (8th) Ⓜ Monceau ♿

Musée Cernuschi (D2) A magnificent collection of Chinese art from its origins to the 13th century, together with contemporary Chinese paintings. The mansion was built for a Milanese businessman, Henri Cernuschi, to house the 5,000 objects he acquired during his travels in Asia. • Daily (except Mon and public holidays) 10am–6pm ☎ 01 53 96 21 50 • 7, av. Velasquez (8th) Ⓜ Villiers, Monceau ♿

Musée Nissim de Camondo (D2) An elegant 18th-century mansion with period furniture and paintings by Mme Vigée-Lebrun, Hubert Robert and others.
• Wed–Sun 10am–5.30pm • 63, rue de Monceau (8th) Ⓜ Villiers

Musée Jacquemart-André (D2) A superb 19th-century town house displaying superb paintings and sculpture of the Italian Renaissance (Mantegna, Bellini, Botticelli, Ucello…), Flemish great masters (Rembrandt, Van Dyck)

French painters and sculptors of the 18th century (Fragonard, Boucher, Vigée Lebrun, Chardin, Greuze). The wall at the top of the magnificent double staircase, above the winter garden, is adorned by a fresco by Tiepolo. Children can join in a treasure hunt; ask for the game book at the reception desk. It's worth getting an audioguide (free). The Café, which opens onto the courtyard, is one of the most exquisite dining rooms in all Paris, hung with tapestries and paintings and furnished with antiques (excellent salads). • Daily 10am–6pm. Café: 11.45am–5.30pm. Sunday brunch from 11am ☎ 01 45 62 11 59 •158 bd Haussmann (8th) Ⓜ St-Philippe-du-Roule ♿

Arc de Triomphe de l'Etoile (C2) After the Battle of Austerlitz, Napoleon had a Triumphal Arch built to the glory of the French army. It took 30 years to build and was inaugurated in 1836, so he never saw it completed. It stands halfway between Place de la Concorde and the Grande Arche at the Défense. From the top (there's a lift) you can admire Baron Haussmann's town planning: 12 wide boulevards radiating out from the arch in the shape of a star. Down below, the cars caught in a never-ending stream of traffic look like little toys. The remains of the Unknown Soldier were buried beneath the arch in 1920 and the eternal flame lit three years later. • Daily, summer 10am–11pm, winter 10am–10.30pm. Ceremony on the Tomb of the Unknown Soldier every evening at 6.30pm • Place Charles-de-Gaulle (8th) Ⓜ ℝℇℝ Charles-de-Gaulle-Etoile

Musée des Arts asiatiques – Guimet (C3) One of the greatest museums of Asian art in the world: splendid collections of Buddhas, paintings, figurines, ceramics and so on, from Afghanistan, India, China, Japan, Thailand, Myanmar beautifully displayed in the completely revamped interior. A short walk away is the Chinese and Japanese Buddhist pantheon, 19, av. d'Iéna, and its small Japanese garden. • Daily (except Tues) 10am–6pm • 6, place d'Iéna (16th) Ⓜ Iéna ℝℇℝ Pont de l'Alma ♿

Musée Baccarat (C3) When the railway reached Paris in the 19th century, the great crystal engravers settled in Rue du Paradis, near the Gare de l'Est, where the creations of the Lorraine factories arrived by train. Baccarat, founded in 1764, is one of the most prestigious of the French cristalliers, with its own museum, and it only recently left Rue du Paradis for the elegant surroundings of the former mansion of Marie-Laure de Noailles. Over a thousand objects from past collections are displayed here, in a decor designed by Philippe Starck. Fine pieces are sold in the shop, and there's another boutique at 11, place de la Madeleine (8th). • **Daily (except Tues, Sun and public holidays) 10am–6.30pm** • 11, place des Etats-Unis (16th) Ⓜ Kléber, Iéna

Musée de la Mode de la Ville de Paris (C3) Temporary exhibitions on fashion through the ages, from the 18th century to the present day. • **Closed for renovation till early 2010** • Palais Galliéra, 10, av. Pierre Ier-de-Serbie (16th) Ⓜ Iéna Ⓡ Pont de l'Alma ♿

Musée d'Art moderne de la Ville de Paris (C3) In the east wing of the Palais de Toyko, 20th-century artworks: murals by Sonia and Robert Delaunay, Matisse, *La Fée Electricité* by Dufy, said to be the biggest painting in the world. Temporary exhibitions. • **Daily (except Mon and public holidays) 10am–6pm, Thurs to 10pm during temporary exhibitions. Free admission.** ☎ 01 53 67 40 00 • 11, av. du Président-Wilson (16th) Ⓜ Iéna Ⓡ Pont de l'Alma

Palais de Tokyo (C3) Contemporary creations, including hands-on exhibits, do-it-yourself graffiti, and so on. • **Daily (except Mon) noon–midnight** • 13, av. du Président-Wilson (16th) Ⓜ Iéna Ⓡ Pont de l'Alma ♿

Palais de Chaillot and Esplanade du Trocadéro (C3) From the terrace of the symmetrical 1930s "palace" the view stretches over the gardens and fountains of the Trocadéro, through the arch of the tower and along the Champ de Mars all the way to the elegant Ecole Militaire, with the golden dome of the Invalides and the curving Y-shaped UNESCO building on the horizon. • **Place du Trocadéro (16th)** Ⓜ Trocadéro

Muséum national d'Histoire naturelle – Musée de l'Homme (C3) Anthropological and prehistoric collections, tracing man's evolution. • **Closed for renovation until 2012** • Palais de Chaillot, 17, place du Trocadéro (16th) Ⓜ Trocadéro ♿

The area around Balzac's house in rue Raynouard has a bucolic atmosphere.

Cité de l'Architecture et du Patrimoine (C3) In the east wing of the Palais de Chaillot, this is the largest centre devoted to architecture in the world. It includes the Institut français d'architecture, the Ecole de Chaillot, and the Musée des Monuments français, whose scale models of great monuments, copies of sculpture, reproductions of wall paintings tell the story of French architecture from the Romanesque era to modern times. • Daily (except Tues and some public holidays) 11am–7pm, Thurs to 9pm ☎ 01 58 51 52 00 • Palais de Chaillot, east wing, 1, place du Trocadéro (16th) Ⓜ Trocadéro

Musée national de la Marine (C3) The history of navigation and maritime transport, fishing, the underwater world, daily life in the arsenals, and so on. Scale models of ships, figureheads, paintings, ancient maps, sextants, compasses and astrolabes and thousands of other nautical objects. • Daily (except Tues, Jan 1, May 1) 10am–6pm ☎ 01 53 65 69 69 • Palais de Chaillot, Passy wing, 17, place du Trocadéro (16th) Ⓜ Trocadéro ♿

Musée du Vin (B4) The vaulted 14th-century cellars of the old Passy abbey, where the monks stored their wine, now house a wine museum which recounts in detail the history of vine cultivation and winemaking. Ancient tools and wax models illustrate the different activities, and the visit is rounded off with a glass of wine. • **Daily (except Mon) 10am–6pm** ☎ 01 45 25 63 26 • Rue des Eaux, 5, square Charles-Dickens (16th) Ⓜ Passy ♿

Maison de Balzac (B4) Around rue Berton, near the banks of the Seine, the 16th arrondissement has retained some of its countrified atmosphere. Next to a pleasant garden opening onto a cobbled, overgrown lane, the mansion where Balzac lived in the 1840s is full of memories of the great writer: his study, portraits and a room of old prints. There's a library and bookshop. Balzac fans will make a pilgrimage to the Vavin métro station in Montparnasse, to see his statue sculpted by Rodin (there's one in the grounds of the Rodin museum, too). • **Daily (except Mon and public holidays) 10am–6pm. Free admission** ☎ 01 55 74 41 80 • 47, rue Raynouard (16th) Ⓜ Passy

Musée Marmottan-Monet (B4) In a splendid 19th-century mansion, objets d'art and furniture of the Renaissance, Consulat and Empire periods, French paintings (Gauguin, Sisley, Renoir, Caillebotte, Pissarro), 100 works by Claude Monet. Regular exhibitions on the Impressionists and Fauves. • **Tues–Sun 11am–6pm, Tues 11am–9pm** • 2, rue Louis-Boilly (16th) Ⓜ La Muette ♿

Bois de Boulogne (A–B 2–5) This huge forest on the western edge of the city is laced with cycle paths and horse trails. Also boating lakes, restaurants, cafés and the Longchamp and Auteuil race courses. Strictly out of bounds after 8pm. In the Parc de Bagatelle, 700 species of rose bloom in summer. Ⓜ Porte Maillot, Porte Dauphine, Porte d'Auteuil

Jardin Shakespeare (A3) The meadow of Pré Catelan has recently been redesigned on the theme of Shakespeare's plays. • Pré Catelan, Bois de Boulogne (16th) Ⓜ Porte Dauphine

Jardin d'Acclimatation (A2) A funfair and well-equipped play area make this a delightful place to take the children. There's a little train, a theatre, the Musée en Herbe, a farm, puppet shows, pony rides and minigolf. Children will love the Hall of Mirrors and Exploradome with its cloud-making machine. • Daily 10am–6pm ☎ 01 40 67 90 82 • Bois de Boulogne (16th) Ⓜ Les Sablons ♿

Parc de Bagatelle (A3) Open-air sculpture exhibitions are presented in this attractively landscaped park, around an 18th-century folly which was the subject of a bet between Marie-Antoinette and her brother-in-law the Comte d'Artois. *"Bagatelle!"* (Fiddlesticks!) he retorted when she defied him to build it in two months. Today you can walk around the rose garden, along the river banks, through the gardens dotted with artificial ruins, or see the exhibitions in the château. • April–Sept 9.30am–8pm, March and Oct to 6.30pm, Nov–Feb to 5pm. Château: mid-April to end Oct, Sun and holidays only from 3pm • Allée de Longchamp Ⓜ Pont de Neuilly, then bus no. 43 or 244 ♿

Grande Arche de la Défense (off map, dir. A1) Clad in white and grey Carrara marble, the Grande Arche towers over the Défense business district. Designed by Johann-Otto von Spreckelsen and inaugurated in 1989 for the Bicentenary of the Revolution, this "window open onto the world" is 110 m high and 106 m wide. Bubble lifts whisk you (for a fee) through the fibreglass "cloud" and up to the terrace. Close by, **Les Quatre Saisons** is a gigantic shopping centre with department stores, boutiques, restaurants and cafés. • Daily, summer 10am–8pm, winter 10am–7pm • 1, parvis de la Défense, 92044 Paris-La-Défense Ⓜ ⓇⒺⓇ La Défense ♿

THE GOLDEN TRIANGLE

For a bout of opulent window-shopping, stroll around the jewellers' and designers' district, a triangle with its apex on place de l'Alma and base on the Champs-Elysées (Vuitton at no. 101). The sides are formed by av. George V (Givenchy at no. 3, Hermès at 42) and av. Montaigne (Christian Dior at no. 30, Chanel at 42). On transversal rue François Ier you'll find Versace at no. 41 and Cartier at no. 51).

WALKING TOUR: TROCADÉRO TO THE CHAMPS-ÉLYSÉES

Just west of the sprawling **Place du Trocadéro**, a statue of Benjamin Franklin sits comfortably at the head of the street bearing his name. Left of Rue Franklin, stairs lead down to the **Jardins du Trocadéro** where ducks swim on a little canal beside the Musée de la Marine. Walk along the gardens' western slope past fire-blackened fragments of the Tuileries Palace and Hôtel de Ville, both burned down by the Paris Communards in 1871. Cross the terrace for a humbling view over the river to the **Eiffel Tower**, and look back at the monstrous **Palais de Chaillot**, built as a cultural centre for the Exposition of 1937 and stylistically not unlike what was being built in Berlin and Moscow.

From the gardens' east exit on Avenue des Nations-Unies, **Avenue d'Iéna** passes the Iranian Embassy (no. 4) and birthplace (no. 10) of Marie Bonaparte, Freudian psychoanalyst and Napoleon's grandniece. On **Place d'Iéna**, George Washington on horseback looks down the avenue of a successor, President Wilson. Across the square, turn right past the **Musée Guimet** along Rue Boissière to Place Marlene Dietrich (identified as "American actress-singer of German origin"). Take **Rue Hamelin** where no. 44 (now Hôtel Elysées Union) was the last home of Marcel Proust who died (in room 511) in 1922. Turn right on Avenue Kléber to **Arc de Triomphe** and Place Charles de Gaulle, still better known as **Place de l'Etoile**.

Start your walk down the **Avenue des Champs-Elysées** by crossing to a traffic island in the middle for a grand view all the way down over the Rond-Point to the Obelisk on Place de la Concorde and the Jardins des Tuileries beyond. Notice the innovative *mobilier urbain* (street furniture) by Jean-Michel Wilmotte—newspaper kiosks, phone booths, lanterns, public benches, bus-stops and traffic lights.

The north, even-numbers side has a predominance of shopping arcades—nos. 84, 76, **Claridge** (FNAC) 74, **Elysées-La Boétie** (Virgin Megastore) 52, and 26. The south, odd-numbers side favours banks and airline offices, but also three venerable cafés, **Fouquet's** (no. 99), **Le Paris** (no. 93) and **Le Deauville** (no. 75), each with its own show-biz clientèle.

CHAMPS-ÉLYSÉES AND THE WEST

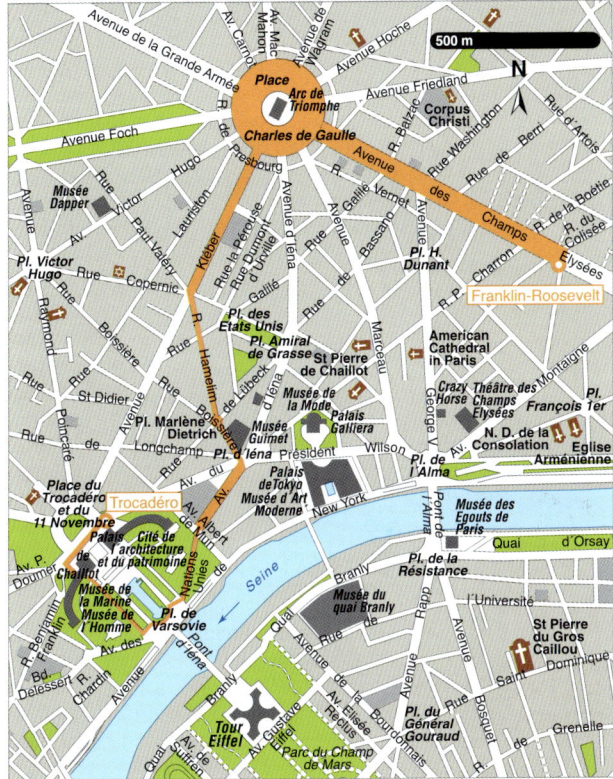

The Trocadéro, a "monumental" part of the posh and residential 16th arrondissement, is just down the road from the Champs-Elysées, the city's flashiest avenue, which boosters insist is the most beautiful in the world.

Start: Ⓜ Trocadéro **Finish:** Ⓜ Franklin-Roosevelt

PARIS ON THE SCREEN

Film—the supreme art form for dreams—and Paris, the city of dreams, were clearly made for each other. Soon after the Lumière brothers put on the world's first public film show on Boulevard des Capucines, on December 28, 1895, pioneer director Georges Méliès was showing the world the Belle Epoque beauties strolling around his Place de l'Opéra. This created an immediate sensation in cinemas opening in London, Berlin and New York, not just for the new phenomenon of film but for the first glimpse it gave ordinary people of Paris's female charmers.

The Dream Works

The dream machine was on its way, rolling inexorably towards such bewitching concoctions as Vincente Minnelli's *American in Paris* (1951). Struggling to make it as a painter, Gene Kelly danced around the Place de la Concorde fountains with lovely Leslie Caron. This was such a hit that Minnelli, Kelly and Caron did it again in 1958 in *Gigi*, this time with views of Montmartre, the Tuileries, Bois de Boulogne and Maxim's restaurant—and Maurice Chevalier doing his cheeky-Frenchman number, Sank 'eaven for Leetle Girls.

The same highly coloured image was projected in John Huston's picture of Toulouse-Lautrec, with José Ferrer on his knees waddling around Montmartre and Pigalle in *Moulin Rouge* (1952).

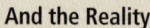

And the Reality

Not feeling a need to push its romantic side, the French presented a more hard-edged view of their capital. Characteristically, Marcel Carné's *Hôtel du Nord* (1938) featuring Louis Jouvet and Arletty became one of France's first cult films with its depiction of pimps, tarts and drunks in the tough 10th arrondissement around Canal Saint-Martin. Arletty's performance as an irresistibly brazen hussy made her a star overnight and added a new rough note to the traditional whore-with-a-heart-of-gold that the world liked to associate with Paris.

Making New Waves
Starting in 1959, the New Wave brought a fresh view of Paris with Jean-Luc Godard's *A Bout de Souffle* (Breathless) in which Jean-Paul Belmondo is a crypto-existentialist gangster, holed up in a Rive Gauche hotel while girlfriend Jean Seberg sells the *International Herald Tribune* on the Champs-Elysées. François Truffaut brought his *Quatre-Cents Coups*, an autobiographical story of boyhood escapades around Place de Clichy, a poignant black and white and grey Montmartre a million light-years away from the Hollywood image. Claude Chabrol's *Les Bonnes Femmes* did the same thing for the unsung area between the Bastille and Place de la République.

Working on his own, Robert Bresson produced with his brilliant *Pickpocket* (also 1959) as bleak a vision of rush-hour Gare de Lyon as any paranoid tourist could dream of.

From One Audrey to Another
Paris was still attracting the foreign crowd. Stanley Donen's crime thriller *Charade* (1963), starring Cary Grant and Audrey Hepburn, is a terrific "tourist guide" to the city—including the Palais Royal, American Express Office, Bateau Mouche, UNESCO—as well as a precious view of the now vanished market-halls of Les Halles. Besides the controversial sexuality of Marlon Brando and Marie Schneider, Bernard Bertolucci's *Last Tango in Paris* (1973) also deals with the vagaries of apartment-hunting in the 16th arrondissement. More nicely romantic is Nancy Meyers' *Something's Gotta Give* (2003) in which Jack Nicholson, Diane Keaton and Keanu Reeves get to share the beauties of Place des Vosges, the Grand Colbert Brasserie and Hôtel de Ville. And then, busting all theories about French compared to American ideas of Paris, there is Jean-Pierre Jeunet's *Le Fabuleux Destin d'Amélie Poulain* (Amélie, 2001). As wide-eyed about Montmartre, Place des Abbesses and all its quaint sidestreets as dear Audrey Tautou herself, the feelgood film to end all feelgood films. The whole world loved it. Why can't Paris always be like that? Dream on.

MONTMARTRE AND THE NORTH

The Romans worked gypsum quarries on the hill that has become Montmartre; in the Middle Ages Benedictine monks planted vines there and built the first windmills. While Montmartre is struggling to retain its village-like atmosphere, the area to the north is undergoing a rapid transformation. In the suburb of Saint-Denis you'll find the Stade de France, and the Royal Necropolis.

THE DISTRICT AT A GLANCE

SIGHTS

Architecture
Basilique du Sacré-Cœur 90

Eglise Saint-Pierre de Montmartre 91

Eglise Saint-Jean de Montmartre 90

Stade de France 92

Basilique de Saint-Denis 93

Atmosphere
Place du Tertre ★ 91

Cimetière de Montmartre 91

Browsing
Marché aux Puces ★ .93

Museums
Espace Montmartre – Salvador Dali 91

Musée de Montmartre ★ 91

Musée de la Vie romantique...............91

Musée Gustave-Moreau 92

WALKING TOUR 94

WINING AND DINING 109

Basilique du Sacré-Cœur (F1) Built as a symbol of penitence after the insurrection of the Commune in 1871, the Sacré-Cœur is made of a special stone that whitens with the contact of carbonic gas in the atmosphere. In Romano-Byzantine style, it was consecrated after World War I. Inside is a large mosaic depicting Christ with outstretched arms. From the dome, you get an exceptional view of the Parisian rooftops. The basilica can be reached by a funicular from the Marché Saint-Pierre (Ⓜ Anvers), or by a long flight of steps. • Daily 6am–11pm. Dome and crypt: summer 9am–6.30pm, winter 9am–5.30pm) ☎ 01 53 41 89 00 • Parvis du Sacré-Cœur (18th) Ⓜ Anvers, Abbesses

Eglise Saint-Pierre de Montmartre (F1) More modest than its gleaming white neighbour, this old church was built in 1147 as part of a great abbey. Inside you can see the tombs of several abbesses, from Adelaide of Savoy, the founder, to Louise-Marie de Montmorency-Laval, beheaded during the Revolution. • **2, rue du Mont-Cenis (18th)** Ⓜ **Abbesses**

Eglise Saint-Jean de Montmartre (E1) Anatole de Baudot used reinforced concrete for this innovative church, with brick and ceramic façade (built 1894–1904). Striking Art Nouveau stained-glass windows. • **19, rue des Abbesses (18th)** Ⓜ **Abbesses**

Place du Tertre (F1) The "village square" of old Montmartre, giving picturesque perspectives of the domes of the Sacré-Cœur. The street artists will immortalize you in charcoal, at a price! Ⓜ **Abbesses**

Espace Montmartre – Salvador Dali (F1) A small museum housing 25 sculptures and 300 engravings, lithographs and illustrations, all the work of the self-styled genius with the upturned moustache. • **Daily 10am–6pm** • **9–11, rue Poulbot (18th)** Ⓜ **Abbesses**

Musée de Montmartre (F1) This 17th-century house was divided up into artist's studios where many famous painters, including Renoir, Dufy, Suzanne Valadon and her son Utrillo, once lived and worked. It has been converted into a museum tracing the colourful history of old Montmartre. • **Daily (except Mon and certain public holidays) 11am–6pm** • **12, rue Cortot (18th)** Ⓜ **Lamarck-Caulaincourt**

Cimetière de Montmartre (E1) The last resting place of Degas, Stendhal, Berlioz, Alfred de Vigny, and, in more recent years, the popular singers Dalida and Michel Berger. • **Daily, summer 8am–6pm, winter 8am–5.30pm** • **Av. Rachel (18th)** Ⓜ **Place de Clichy**

Musée de la Vie romantique (E1) This delightfully romantic retreat is suprisingly set in the red-light district of Pigalle. The house was the last home of the Dutch painter Ary Scheffer, a member of the French Romantic school and friend of Ingres, Delacroix, Lamartine, Chopin and George Sand. Temporary exhibitions. The ground floor is devoted to George Sand, and there's a pleasant tea-room in the conservatory. • **Daily (except Mon and public holidays) 10am–6pm** ☎ 01 55 31 95 67 • 16, rue Chaptal (9th) Ⓜ Blanche, St-Georges

Musée Gustave-Moreau (E2) Time has stood still in the studio of this Symbolist painter, master of Matisse and Rouault, since his death in 1898. You can see his most famous painting, *Jupiter et Sémélé*, and numerous other works in a style mingling lyricism and mythology. Known as Nouvelle-Athènes, the neighbouring district centred on rue de la Tour-des-Dames was given its name in the 1820s when neoclassical houses were built for famous actors of the time. • **Daily (except Tues) 10am–12.45pm and 2–5.15pm** ☎ 01 48 74 38 50 • 14, rue de La Rochefoucauld (9th) Ⓜ Trinité

Stade de France (off map, dir. D1) It's great to go for a football match or concert, but if you're an architecture buff you might also like to discover the fascinating secrets of this splendid stadium. • **Daily 10am–6pm, except during**

THE REAL MONTMARTRE

Escape from place du Tertre and explore the residential streets, where you'll discover splendid villas, artist's studios (look for the big windows) and quiet squares. The Bateau-Lavoir studio on Place Emile-Goudeau, where Picasso, Braque and Juan Gris developed Cubism, has been replaced by a block of flats, but photos in the windows show the squalid conditions in which the artists once worked. Climb steep Rue Lepic (Amélie's bar-tabac des Deux-Moulins is at no. 15), then explore Avenue Junot with its Dadaist houses and gardens, and Villa Léandre swathed in greenery. See the sculpture by Jean Marais of a man emerging from a wall (the main character of Marcel Aymé's novel *Passe-Muraille*). Rue des Abbesses is full of busy cafés. In autumn, don't miss the wine harvest in the little vineyard on the corner of rues St-Vincent and Saules. The wine is auctioned and the profits given to a charity. Lower down, the 19th-century cabarets of Pigalle have been replaced by nightclubs and sex shops.

matches or concerts (entrance gate J). Guided tours in English daily at 2.30pm, in French 10am–5pm ☎ 08 92 70 09 00 • Saint-Denis – Porte de Paris Ⓡ Stade de France ♿

Basilique de Saint-Denis – Nécropole royale (off map, dir. G1) The kings of France were buried in this basilica from the 7th century onwards. You can see numerous tombs and recumbent statues, some of them striking. Don't miss the Gallo-Roman museum. • Apr–Sept Mon–Sat 10am–6.15pm, Sun noon–6.15pm; Oct–March Mon–Sat 10am–5.15pm, Sun noon–5.15pm ☎ 01 48 09 83 54 • 1, rue de la Légion d'Honneur Ⓜ Basilique de St-Denis

Marché aux Puces (off map, dir. E–F1) The bargains are snapped up quickly, so get to the flea market as early as you can. Walk right past the stalls selling T-shirts, sneakers and so on until you get to the real flea market, heralded by a banner. Seven distinct markets cover the range from *brocante* (second-hand goods) to *antiquités* (the real thing). **Paul-Bert** is best for rustic or bistro furniture, antique dolls. **Biron** deals in genuine antiques. **Malik** sells clothes in every style. **Serpette**, the trendiest, for early-20th-century furniture. **Jules-Vallès**, the cheapest bric-à-brac. **Vernaison** specializes in furniture, ornaments and silverware. **Vallès-Lécuyer** for Art Deco objects, designer clothes and objects, army surplus. Sat 9am–6pm, Sun 10am–6pm, Mon 11am–5pm • Porte de Saint-Ouen (18th) Ⓜ Porte de Clignancourt

WALKING TOUR: THE VILLAGE OF MONTMARTRE

Place Jules Joffrin is immediately evocative of Montmartre's provincial village atmosphere, between the lofty 19th-century Eglise Notre-Dame-de-Clignancourt and the **Mairie du 18e Arrondissement**, monumental epitome of civic pride in the Third Republic.

To the right of the town hall, take **Rue Mont Cenis**. At no. 63. the pepperpot tower dates back at least to 1480 and is now part of a nightclub. Turn right along Rue Marcadet and left on Rue de la Fontaine du But to a double staircase embracing the entrance to métro Lamarck-Caulaincourt.

At the top of the stairs on Place Constantin Pecqueur, follow the signpost left on Rue Lucien Gaillard—unusual rear view of Sacré Cœur—to **Cimetière Saint-Vincent** with its early 19th-century tomb sculptures. In the far left hand corner is the red marble tomb of painter Maurice Utrillo. Also buried here are composer Arthur Honegger and writer Marcel Aymé.

Back on Place Constantin Pecqueur, turn left on Rue Saint-Vincent behind the cemetery to the cabaret **Au Lapin Agile**, favourite of Verlaine, Renoir, Apollinaire and Picasso. On the right is the **Clos-Montmartre vineyard** and further along Rue Saint-Vincent the lovely **Jardin sauvage Saint-Vincent**, a terraced garden for flowers growing wild in a biotope that attracts otherwise rare birds and insects.

Double back and turn left up Rue des Saules to the Maison Rose, home of Utrillo. Take Rue de l'Abreuvoir down to **Place Dalida** with its busty bronze bust of the Egyptian-born French pop singer (1933–1987).

Allée des Brouillards passes an 18th-century château and several pretty houses and gardens to Place Casadesus. Beyond, on the left, is **Square Suzanne Buisson**, a popular garden with a statue of Saint Denis where the martyr stopped to wash his severed head in a fountain.

Exit from the garden's upper terrace and turn right on **Avenue Junot** with its many fine mansions, notably no. 15, Viennese architect Adolf Loos' white cubist house for Dada poet Tristan Tzara. Double back to cross Place Marcel Aymé, turn right on Rue d'Orchampt to end up at Place Emile Goudeau, where Picasso and Braque shared the **Bateau-Lavoir studios** (burned down in 1970), and a grand view over Paris.

MONTMARTRE AND THE NORTH

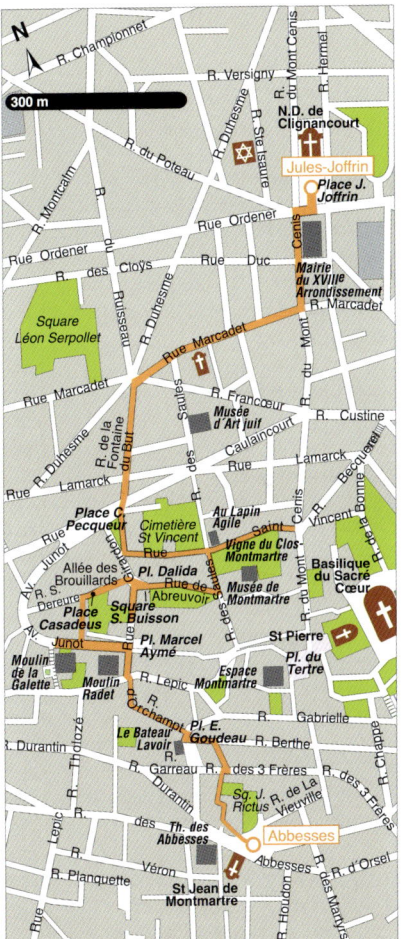

Away from the tourist haunts, Montmartre is a village of gardens, vineyards, elegant mansions and artists' studios, up- and downhill on the Mons Martyrum.

Start:
Ⓜ Jules Joffrin

Finish:
Ⓜ Abbesses

AROUND PARIS

Why restrict yourself to the big city sights, when there's so much to see in the outskirts? These are popular day trips, most of the destinations easily reached by RER train.

Château de Vincennes The castle was a royal residence from the 12th to 18th centuries. It still has its fortifications, its medieval towers and imposing 14th-century keep, 50 m high. It has all been beautifully restored. Also see the pavillions of the king and the queen, built by Le Vau in the 17th century. • Daily May–Aug 10am–6pm, Sept–Apr 10am–5pm. Closed some public holidays. ☎ 01 48 08 31 20 • Avenue de Paris, 94300 Vincennes Ⓜ ⓇⒺⓇ line A to Vincennes

Châteaux de Malmaison and Bois-Préau Empress Josephine, wife of Napoleon Bonaparte, bought the château at Malmaison in 1799 and lived there until she died in 1814. The rooms are full of souvenirs of Napoleon's boyhood and Josephine's personal belongings. The neighbouring château of Bois-Préau has been turned into a museum documenting Napoleon's exile on the island of St Helena (closed for renovation till 2010). • Daily (except Tues), Oct–March 10am–12.30pm, 1.30–5.15pm; Sat, Sun 10am–5.45pm; Apr–Aug 10am–5.45pm, Sat, Sun 10am–6.15pm ☎ 01 41 29 05 55 • 1, av. du Château, 92500 Rueil-Malmaison ⓇⒺⓇ line A to Rueil-Malmaison, then bus no. 258

Disneyland Resort Paris Two theme parks, Disneyland and Walt Disney Studios, hotels, golf course and Disney Village (shops, bars, restaurants, wild west show and multiplex cinema. At nearby Val d'Europe, the SeaLife aquarium in a sparkling new shopping mall, and La Vallée Outlet Shopping Village. • Hours vary; check beforehand ☎ 08 25 30 60 30 • 77777 Marne-la-Vallée ⓇⒺⓇ Line A direction Marne-la-Vallée/Chessy; terminus: Chessy. Trains every 20 minutes. Last train for Paris (direction St-Germain-en-Laye) at 00.20 ♿

Parc Astérix In their village in the Gaul's Forest, France's immortal comic-strip heroes Asterix, Obelix and the druid Getafix are still holding out against Roman attack, with a little help from the druid's magic potion. Theme park with shows, shops, restaurants, performing dolphins and seals. Picnicking allowed. • Open April to October; for days and times see calendar on www.parcasterix.fr ☎ 08 26 30 10 40 • 60128 Plailly ⓇⒺⓇ Line B3 – Roissy-Charles de Gaulle, then shuttle bus. A1 motorway ♿

Giverny: Fondation Claude Monet It takes an effort to reach Giverny, and you'll only see photographic reproductions of Monet's paintings in his house and studio. But no one is disappointed by the Japanese water garden complete with weeping willows, wooden bridges and waterlilies. • Daily (except Mon) 9.30am–6pm (last tickets 5.30pm) ☎ 02 32 51 28 21 • 27620 Giverny • Train: SNCF Gare Saint-Lazare (trains for Rouen) to Vernon, then bus, taxi or bicycle the 7 km (4 miles) to Giverny. ♿

Giverny: Musée des Impressionismes The former Museum of American Art displays works by the small colony of American artists—Willard Metcalf, Louis Ritter, Theodor Wendel, John Leslie Breck and others—who lived in Giverny at the same time as Monet. Temporary exhibitions are organized, and the gardens are worth a visit. There is also a café with independant entrance. • Daily May–Oct 10am–6pm during exhibitions ☎ 02 32 51 94 65 • 99, rue Claude Monet, 27620 Giverny • Directions as above ♿

Château de Chantilly: Musée Condé The castle of Chantilly houses a prestigious collection of Old Masters such as Raphael, Poussin and Watteau. In the library, admire the famous illuminated Book of Hours, *Les Très Riches Heures du Duc de Berry*, depicting minute details of medieval life. • Daily (except Tues) 10am–6pm. Park: daily (except Tues) 10am–dusk. ☎ 03 44 62 62 62 • 60631 Chantilly ⓇⒺⓇ Line D – Chantilly

Château de Chantilly: Musée Vivant du Cheval Equestrian shows are presented in the superb 18th-century Grandes Ecuries (Great Stables), commissioned by Louis-Henri de Bourbon, Prince of Condé, who believed he would be reincarnated as a horse. • April–Oct Mon, Wed–Fri 10.30am–5.30pm; Sat, Sun and public holidays 10.30am–6pm; Nov–Mar Mon, Wed–Fri 2–5pm; Sat, Sun, holidays 10.30am–5.30pm. Dressage demonstrations at varying times ☎ 03 44 57 40 40 • 60631 Chantilly ⓇⒺⓇ Line D – Chantilly

Château de Versailles Take a full day to visit the extravagant home of the kings of France, from Louis XIV (1678) to Louis XVI (1789). With all their gilt, marble, crystal, paintings and tapestries, the grand apartments are overwhelming, perfectly matching the vainglorious character of the Sun King, Louis XIV. The mirror-lined Galerie des Glaces has been beautifully restored. Studded with statues, refreshed by ponds and fountains, the gardens are a delight. Take the little train or a horse-drawn carriage, or walk to the more modest Grand and Petit Trianon palaces, and Marie-Antoinette's "hamlet" in the woods, where the Queen dressed as a dairymaid to "return to nature". Some areas are being restored. The castle is a 5-minute walk from the métro station. • Daily (except Mon and public holidays), summer 9am–6.30pm, winter 9am–5.30pm. Grand Trianon and Petit Trianon: summer noon–6.30pm, winter noon–5.30pm; last entry 30 min before closing. ☏ 01 30 83 78 00. Fountains: summer Sat, Sun 11am–noon, 3.30–5pm, 5.20–5.30pm ☏ 01 30 83 78 89 • 78000 Versailles Ⓜ Pont de Sèvres, then bus 171, ⓇⒺⓇ Line C – Versailles RG ♿

Château de Fontainebleau The kings of France used to come to Fontainebleau to hunt in the great forest. François I built the palace in 1527 on the site of a hunting lodge, and it became the artistic centre of the French Renaissance. There's a museum devoted to Napoleon I and his family in the Louis XV wing, a Renaissance Gallery and a magnificent library. • Daily (except Tues and certain public holidays) 9.30am–6pm in summer, 9.30am–5pm in winter ☏ 01 60 71 50 70 • 77300 Fontainebleau. Train: SNCF Gare de Lyon to Fontainebleau-Avon, then bus ♿

Vaux-le-Vicomte Louis XIV threw a fit when he saw the splendid château that his Finance Minister Nicolas Fouquet had built for himself. Fouquet was thrown into gaol, and the king commissioned the Vaux-le-Vicomte architects Le Vau, Le Brun and Le Nôtre to build an even grander castle at Versailles. • Daily, summer 10am–6pm (closed Wed except July–Aug); candlelight tours Fri in July and August and Sat May–Oct 8–midnight (last admission 11pm). ☏ 01 64 14 41 90 • 77950 Maincy ⓇⒺⓇ ligne D – Melun, then taxi (7 km) or Chateaubus shuttle Sat, Sun and holidays mid-June–Sept, approx. every hour from 10.25, last departure from the château at 5.50pm ♿

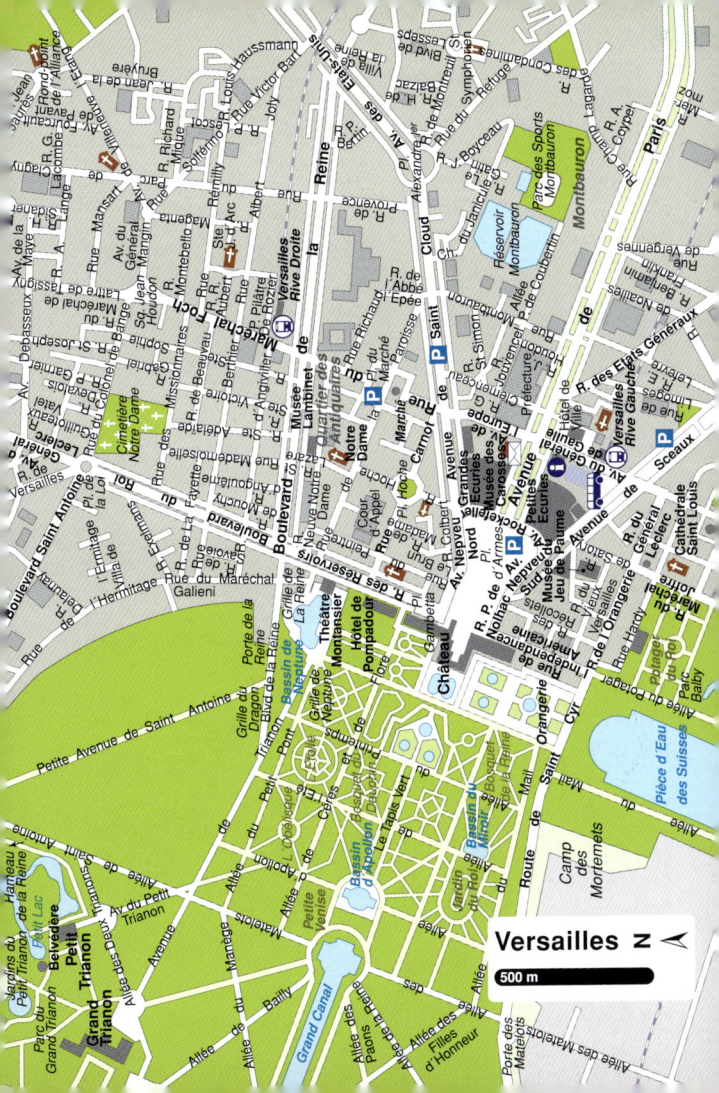

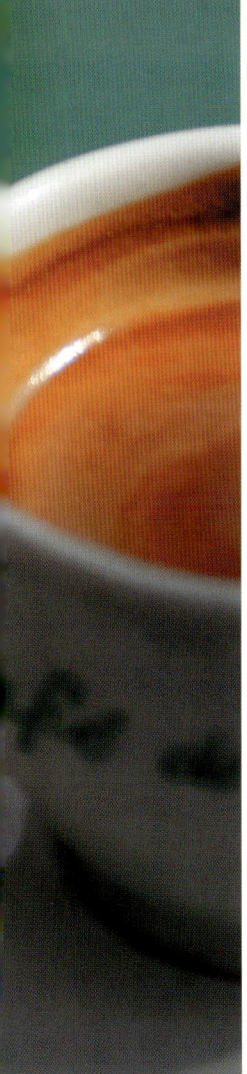

cityBites

The food scene is changing, becoming more international and democratic. The number of fast-food outlets, self-services and sandwich bars is on the increase. Note that since January 2008, smoking is forbidden in all public places.

Don't fall into the trap of "tourist menus": the French fries may be all right but you're bound to be disappointed by the steak. Our listing provides a selection of restaurants, brasseries, bistros and cafés where you are sure to eat well. Prices (excluding wine) are coded:

- 1 up to 20 euros;
- 2 up to 45 euros;
- 3 over 45 euros;
- 4 the sky's the limit

Unless stated otherwise, the restaurants listed are open on weekends (but they often close for a month in July and August). Most places offer a fixed-price menu, service charge included (*service compris*).

THE ISLANDS AND THE SEINE

La Taverne Henry IV
Ⓜ Pont-Neuf
13, pl. du Pont-Neuf (1st)
☎ 01 43 54 27 90
Mon–Fri noon–10pm, Sat lunch only. Closed all Sun
[2]

Excellent wines and tasty regional dishes such as *tripous* (tripe with mutton shank). Sandwiches, pâtés, cheeses for lunch.

Le Vieux Bistro
Ⓜ Cité
14, rue du Cloître-Notre-Dame (4th)
☎ 01 43 54 18 95
Daily noon–2.30pm and 7–10.30pm
[2]

Popular bistro serving excellent French cuisine. Authentic décor.

LATIN QUARTER

Au Buisson ardent
Ⓜ Jussieu
25, rue de Jussieu (5th)
☎ 01 43 54 93 02
Closed Sat lunch and all Sun
[1]

Regional produce in unusual yet tasty combinations.

Chez Léna et Mimile
Ⓜ Place Monge
32, rue Tournefort (5th)
☎ 01 47 07 72 47
Daily noon–2.30pm and 7–11pm
[2]

Quaint and romantic décor, like a postcard of old Paris, overlooking a garden. Classic cuisine.

Le Grenier de Notre-Dame
Ⓜ St Michel
18, rue de la Bûcherie (5th)
☎ 01 43 29 98 29
[1]

Perfect for vegetarians: the "attic" serves traditional French dishes but meat-free: *cassoulet* (beans), *choucroute* with soya sausages, lentil moussaka, and so on.

Perraudin
🚇 Luxembourg
157, rue St-Jacques (5th)
☎ 01 46 33 15 75
Daily 9am–10pm
No credit cards
[1]

A friendly old bistro providing simple, long-simmered home-style cooking.

Les Cinq Saveurs d'Anada
Ⓜ Cardinal-Lemoine
72, rue Cardinal-Lemoine (5th)

Brasserie Lipp

☎ 01 43 29 58 54
Closed Mon
[1]

Biological cuisine, tending towards the macrobiotic: fish, vegetables, tempeh, tofu.

Tashi Delek
Ⓜ Luxembourg
4, rue des Fossés-St-Jacques (5th)
☎ 01 43 26 55 55
Closed Sun
[1]

For an exotic gastronomic experience, taste a selection of Regional Tibetan dishes, prepared by authentic Tibetans.

La Tour d'Argent
Ⓜ Pont-Marie
15–17, quai de la Tournelle (5th)
☎ 01 43 54 23 31
Closed Sun and Mon
Book well ahead
[4]

Gastronomic restaurant with a superb view over the Seine.

SAINT-GERMAIN MONTPARNASSE

Café de Flore
Ⓜ St-Germain-des-Prés
172, bd St-Germain (6th)
☎ 01 45 48 55 26
Daily 7.30am–1.30pm
[2]

It became famous in the days of Existentialism, when Simone de Beauvoir and Jean-Paul Sartre came here to keep warm.

Casa Bini
Ⓜ Odéon
36, rue Grégoire de Tours (6th)
☎ 01 46 34 05 60
Daily 12.30–2.30pm and 7.30–11pm
Reservation advised.
[2]

Excellent Tuscan cuisine, linguini with crab *(tourteau)* or truffles, in season. You may recognize some TV or movie stars among the clientèle beneath the wooden beams.

La Closerie des Lilas
🄬 Port-Royal
171, bd du Montparnasse (6th)
☎ 01 40 51 34 50
Open to 1am
[3]

Hemingway used to hang out in this café, along with Alfred Jarry, Paul Fort, not to mention Lenin and other revolutionaries. Budding writers still come for inspiration.

Les Deux Magots
Ⓜ St-Germain-des-Prés
6, pl. St-Germain-des-Prés (6th)
☎ 01 45 48 55 25
Daily 7.30am–1am
[2]

Writers Camus, Jacques Prévert and Sartre scribbled their first lines within the walls of this café.

Forêt noire
Ⓜ Odéon
9, rue de l'Eperon (6th)
☎ 01 44 41 00 09
Tues–Sat from noon
[1]

Light dishes such as quiche and salad, in a haven of peace just off Saint-Germain. Sunday brunch.

La Jacobine
Ⓜ Odéon
59–61, rue St-André-des-Arts (6th)
☎ 01 46 34 15 95
Daily (except Mon) noon–11pm
[1]

Tea room during the day serving buckwheat pancakes, hot open sandwiches on Poilâne bread, fruit tarts. Evenings: good salads, fine cuisine.

Le Procope

Lipp
Ⓜ St-Germain-des-Prés
151, bd St-Germain (6th)
☎ 01 45 48 53 91
Daily to 00.45am
[2]

Famous literary brasserie with Belle Epoque décor in the heart of Saint-Germain. People come more for the atmosphere than for the food, which is fairly classic.

Le Procope
Ⓜ Odéon
13, rue de l'Ancienne-Comédie (6th)
☎ 01 40 46 79 00
Daily noon–midnight
[2]

It claims to be the oldest café in Paris, founded in 1686 by Francesco Procopio dei Coltelli from Palermo. The food is good and the historic décor very attractive.

Au Sauvignon
Ⓜ Sèvres-Babylone
80, rue des Saints-Pères (7th)
☎ 01 45 48 49 02
[1]

Cosy wine bar, its walls covered with caricatures. Delicious open sandwiches (*tartines*).

Au Vin des Rues
Ⓜ Denfert-Rochereau
21, rue Boulard (14th)
☎ 01 43 22 19 78
Open daily for lunch and dinner except Sun lunch
No credit cards
[2]
The hearty cuisine of Lyon, which involves lots of onion and potatoes.

La Coupole
Ⓜ Vavin
102, bd du Montparnasse (14th)
☎ 01 43 20 14 20
Daily from 8.30am; last orders (brasserie) at 1am (Fri and Sat 1.30am)
[2]
The Coupole is a Parisian institution, and has been the rendezvous of artists and intellectuals ever since it was opened in 1927. At the time it was the biggest café in Paris. Local artists were commissioned for the paintings on the pillars, their salary amounting to credit for unlimited drinks.

Le Dôme
Ⓜ Vavin
108, bd du Montparnasse (14th)
☎ 01 43 35 25 81
Last orders 11.30pm
[3]
In the 1920s, the Surrealists used to meet up here or at La Coupole. The café later became one of the haunts of Simone de Beauvoir and Jean-Paul Sartre. Today, the restaurant is one of the best places in Paris for fish and shellfish.
The neighbouring bistro, at no. 1 rue Delambre, has the same proprietor, but the food is easier on the wallet.

INVALIDES AND EIFFEL TOWER

Au Petit Tonneau
Ⓜ Invalides
20, rue de Surcouf (7th)
☎ 01 47 05 09 01
[1]
Classic French cuisine with a lady chef at the helm.

Au Pied de Fouet
Ⓜ Sèvres-Babylone
rue de Babylone (7th)
☎ 01 47 05 12 27
[2]
Excellent value for money in this friendly restaurant with an authentic zinc bar.

Le Jules Verne
Ⓜ Bir-Hakeim
🅁🄴🅁 Champ-de-Mars
2nd floor of the Eiffel Tower (7th)
☎ 01 45 55 61 44
[4]
Priceless cuisine, an unforgettable view over Paris by night. Book well ahead – a few days for lunch, a few months for weekend dinner.

LOUVRE AND PALAIS ROYAL

Café Marly
Ⓜ Palais-Royal
Palais du Louvre,
Cour Napoléon,
93, rue de Rivoli (1st)
☎ 01 49 26 06 60
Daily to 2am
[2]
Smart café overlooking the pyramid, in the arcades of the Louvre. The décor is at once classical and modern; people come here to see and to be seen. Shaded terrace. Gourmets rave over its mashed potatoes.

Le Grand Véfour
Ⓜ Palais-Royal
17, rue de Beaujolais (1st)
☎ 01 42 96 56 27
Closed Frid evening, Sat, Sun and all August
[4]
Founded in 1760, this is considered one of the best addresses in Paris and has long been the haunt of writers and politicians. It looks out

Le Grand Colbert

over the Palais-Royal gardens and is listed as a historic monument. Chef Guy Martin concocts a refined cuisine; exceptional wine list.

L'Incroyable
Ⓜ Palais-Royal–Musée du Louvre
26, rue de Richelieu (1st)
Another entrance at
23, rue de Montpensier
☎ 01 42 96 24 64
②

A friendly little restaurant hidden down a narrow alley close to the Palais-Royal. The building dates from 1643. A few tables are set up outside in summer. Unpretentious French food such as *confit d'oie* (preserved goose) with sautéed potatoes, *andouillette* (tripe sausage), veal liver *(foie de veau)* with blackcurrant sauce, and delicious fruit *clafoutis* for dessert.

Le Véro Dodat
Ⓜ Louvre-Rivoli
19, galerie Véro-Dodat (1st)
☎ 01 45 08 92 06
Closed Sun, and Mon evening
②

Ideal if it's raining: you can still dine on the terrace, in one of the most beautiful arcades in Paris.

Le Grand Colbert
Ⓜ Richelieu-Drouot
2–4, rue Vivienne (2nd)
☎ 01 42 86 87 88
Open daily noon–1am
②

Handsome brasserie in the Galerie Colbert; the fish soup and *bœuf gros sel* are highly acclaimed.

Le Vaudeville
Ⓜ Bourse
29, rue Vivienne (2nd)
☎ 01 40 20 04 62
②

Classic brasserie fare in an Art Déco setting, popular for after-theatre dinner. Specialities include *choucroute*, fish, shellfish.

LES HALLES LE MARAIS

A la Tour de Montlhéry
Ⓜ Louvre–Rivoli
ⓇⒺⓇ Châtelet–Les Halles
5, rue des Prouvaires (1st)
☎ 01 42 36 21 82
Open day and night except Sat and Sun
②

Familiarly known as Chez Denise, this is a veritable institution in the Halles area. Good meat dishes and terrines.

Au Pied de Cochon
Ⓜ Louvre–Rivoli
ⓇⒺⓇ Châtelet–Les Halles
6, rue Coquillère (1st)
☎ 01 40 13 77 00
24-hour service
②

If you fancy a grilled pig's trotter, a good onion soup, some delicious seafood, or just a taste of the authentic Parisian atmosphere, this is the right place for you.

Le Louchébem
Ⓜ Châtelet
31, rue Berger (1st)
☎ 01 42 33 12 99
Closed Sun
①

Grilled meat, incredibly tender, and very big portions. The chef was a butcher so knows what he's cooking. The name is a butcher's slang version of "Butcher".

Saudade
Ⓜ Louvre–Rivoli
ⓇⒺⓇ Châtelet–Les Halles
34, rue des Bourdonnais (1st)
☎ 01 42 36 30 71
Closed Sun
②

Gastronomic Portuguese cuisine in a cool and elegant atmosphere. It is

Bofinger

considered by those in the know to be the best Portuguese restaurant in the capital.

A la Grille Montorgueil
Ⓜ Les Halles
50, rue Montorgueil(2nd)
☎ 01 42 33 21 21
Daily, last orders at 00.30am
[2]

Traditional bistro food in a pedestrian street. Blackboard menu.

Le Tambour
Ⓜ Les Halles, Sentier
41, rue Montmartre (2nd)
☎ 01 42 33 06 90
Tues–Sat noon–3pm, daily 6pm–6am
[1]

Folksy bistrot, decorated with old métro signs and sewer lids. Traditional cuisine (*andouillette* and so on) .

Auberge Nicolas Flamel
Ⓜ Rambuteau
51, rue de Montmorency (3th)
☎ 01 42 71 77 78
Open Mon–Sat, Sun by reservation
[2]

Gastronomic cuisine in one of the oldest houses in Paris, the former home of a 15th-century alchemist. A speciality: the melt-in-the-mouth *gigot de 7 heures* (leg of lamb slowly baked for seven hours).

Au Vin des Pyrénées
Ⓜ Bastille, St Paul
25, rue Beautreillis (4th)
☎ 01 42 72 64 94
Closed Sat lunch. Sunday brunch
[2]

You'll get a friendly welcome in this informal bar with a simple lunch menu of grilled meat or fish with copious side dishes. Wine by the glass.

Bofinger
Ⓜ Bastille
5, rue de la Bastille (4th)
☎ 01 42 72 87 82
[2]

Traditional brasserie with glorious Belle Epoque décor. Book ahead. People in the know ask for the table under the pretty dome (*sous la coupole*). Excellent cuisine, attentive service (Flo group).

L'Enoteca
Ⓜ St-Paul
25, rue Charles V (4th)
☎ 01 42 78 91 44
[1]

The cuisine of Northern Italy. Superb wine cellar with bottles from every region.

Ma Bourgogne
Ⓜ St-Paul
19, pl. des Vosges (4th)
☎ 01 42 78 44 64
[2]

Traditional cuisine and hand-picked wines, beneath the arcades.

La Tartine
Ⓜ St-Paul
24, rue de Rivoli (4th)
☎ 01 42 72 76 85
Closed Tues, and Wed morning
[1]

Wine bar with excellent cheese or charcuterie sandwiches.

BASTILLE, BERCY

Le Dôme Bastille
Ⓜ Bastille
2, rue de la Bastille (4th)
☎ 01 48 04 88 44
Book ahead
[2]

One of the best fish restaurants in the whole of Paris. Straight from the sea and into your plate.

Chez Paul
Ⓜ Ledru-Rollin
13, rue de Charonne (11th)

☎ 01 47 00 34 57
2

This must be one of the most popular restaurants of the Bastille area. The slightly moth-eaten atmosphere is carefully nurtured. Book ahead if you want a chance of finding a table for lunch.

Paris Main d'Or
Ⓜ Ledru-Rollin
133, rue du Faubourg-St-Antoine (11th)
☎ 01 44 68 04 68
Closed Sun
Book ahead
2

Corsican atmosphere and savours, bilingual French-Corsican Menu.

A la Biche au Bois
Ⓜ Gare de Lyon
45, av. Ledru-Rollin(12th)
☎ 01 43 43 34 38
Closed Sat, Sun, and Mon lunch.
Book ahead.
2 ♿

Country cooking, excellent value for money. Terrines, home-made desserts.

L'Ebauchoir
Ⓜ Faidherbe-Chaligny, Reuilly-Diderot
43, rue de Cîteaux (12th)
☎ 01 43 42 49 31
Closed Sun and Mon
1

Friendly bistrot with wooden tables, offering

Le Train Bleu

good, traditional food and excellent value for money. Menu on a slate.

Le Train Bleu
Ⓜ Gare de Lyon
Gare de Lyon –
20, bd Diderot (12th)
☎ 01 43 43 09 06
Book well ahead
3

It's expensive, but worth every centime if just to sit on the leather couches in a palatial setting. There's no other station buffet like this one, a historic monument, and the perfect place to while away the hours while waiting for your train. Cuisine "bourgeoise".

GRANDS BOULEVARDS

Tavern'Café
Ⓜ Richelieu-Drouot
17–19, bd Montmartre (2nd)
☎ 01 42 61 82 88
Open daily
1

A brasserie and tea room near the Musée Grévin.

Good food, a literary décor, and wi-fi connection.

Bistrot du Sommelier
Ⓜ St-Augustin
97, bd Haussmann (8th)
☎ 01 42 65 24 85
Closed Sat and Sun
2

Wine bar reclassified as a wine restaurant, for connoisseurs. Menus based on fresh, seasonal produce from the local market—what they call *cuisine du marché*.

Ladurée
Ⓜ Madeleine, Concorde
16, rue Royale (8th)
☎ 01 42 60 21 79
Mon–Thurs
8.30am–7.30pm,
Sat 8.30am–8pm,
Sun 10am–7pm
1

Next to the pâtisserie (famous for its chocolate macaroons), a tea room serving a light cuisine in a beautiful, old-fashioned décor; many kinds of tea. Other branches at 75, av. des Champs-Elysées, 21, rue Bonaparte and in the Printemps department store.

Chartier
Ⓜ Grands Boulevards
7, rue du Faubourg-Montmartre (9th)
☎ 01 47 70 86 29

Open daily
[1]
A cheerful, noisy place with good, basic food. This historic monument seats 1,300.

Goûtu
Ⓜ Le Peletier
51, rue Le Peletier (9th)
☎ 01 44 79 01 87
Mon–Fri 11am–4pm
[1]
No less than 30 kinds of freshly made sandwiches from 1 to 3 euros.

Le Relais Savoyard
Ⓜ Notre-Dame de Lorette, Cadet
13, rue Rodier (9th)
☎ 01 45 26 17 48
[1]
Succulent dishes typical of the French Savoie region.

Le Roi du Pot-au-Feu
Ⓜ Havre-Caumartin
34, rue Vignon (9th)
☎ 01 47 42 37 10
Closed Sun
[2]
Nothing but *pot au feu* (boiled beef and vegetables) in three versions: poor, medium class (with dessert), and rich (with broth and dessert). No bookings.

Julien
Ⓜ Strasbourg–St-Denis
16, rue du Faubourg-St-Denis (10th)
☎ 01 47 70 12 06
Open daily
[2]
Classic French cuisine in this superb Art Nouveau brasserie, which started life as a *bouillon* (a soup kitchen).

CHAMPS-ÉLYSÉES AND THE WEST

Le Bœuf sur le Toit
Ⓜ St-Philippe-du-Roule
34, rue du Colisée (8th)
☎ 01 53 93 65 55
[2]
Very busy brasserie belonging to the Flo chain. Magnificent 1930s décor, attentive service.

La Fermette Marbeuf 1900
Ⓜ Alma-Marceau
5, rue Marbeuf (8th)
☎ 01 53 23 08 00
Book 4–5 days ahead
[2]
Exquisite Art Nouveau setting and classic cuisine.

Le Fouquet's-Barrière
Ⓜ George-V
99, av. des Champs-Elysées (8th)
☎ 01 47 23 70 60
Daily to 1am
[3]
A Champs-Elysées institution. Everyone that's someone comes to Fouquet's.

Julien

Lasserre
Ⓜ Champs-Elysées-Clémenceau
17, av. Franklin-D.-Roosevelt (8th)
☎ 01 43 59 53 43
Every evening, as well as Thurs and Fri lunch.
Closed Sun
[4]
A symbol of the Parisian art de vivre. The roof opens to let you sit beneath the shady trees. Irreproachable cuisine and service, in keeping with the prices.

Taillevent
Ⓜ George-V
15, rue Lamennais (8th)
☎ 01 44 95 15 01
Closed Sat and Sun
[4]
Gastronomic restaurant with beautifully decorated rooms, and a cellar with over 300,000 bottles.

Le Petit Rétro
Ⓜ Victor-Hugo
5, rue Mesnil (16th)
☎ 01 44 05 06 05
Closed Sat and Sun
[2]

An attractive and friendly little bistro offering no-nonsense cooking.

Ecole de Paris des Métiers de la Table
Ⓜ Louise-Michel
17, rue Jacques Albert (17th)
☎ 01 44 09 12 16
Closed Sat and Sun
[1]

At lunchtime you can sample the fine dishes prepared by the students and chefs of this renowned hotel school, at very low prices.

Restaurant L'Entredgeu
Ⓜ Porte de Champerret
83, rue de Laugier (17th)
☎ 01 40 54 97 24
Closed Sat and Sun. Fixed-price blackboard menu
[2]

Tiny bistro with even tinier kitchen, serving excellent food, good value.

MONTMARTRE AND THE NORTH

Charlot
Ⓜ Clichy
81, bd de Clichy (9th)
☎ 01 53 20 48 00
Mon–Fri to midnight, Sat and Sun to 1 am
[2]

Charlot the shellfish king holds court in a renowned fish restaurant.

Le Bourgogne
Ⓜ Jacques Bonsergent
Chez Maurice
26, rue des Vinaigriers (10th)
☎ 01 46 07 07 91
Closed Sat lunch and Sun
[1]

Small old-fashioned restaurant serving home cooking, near the Saint-Martin canal and the Hôtel du Nord.

Flo
Ⓜ Château d'Eau
7, cour des Petites-Ecuries (10th)
☎ 01 47 70 13 59
[2]

Founded back in 1886 as a beer warehouse, this brasserie is especially famed for shellfish.

Terminus Nord
Ⓜ Gare du Nord
23, rue de Dunkerque (10th)
☎ 01 42 85 05 15
[2]

Good shellfish and superb cuisine in Art Deco surroundings.

Aux Négociants
Ⓜ Château-Rouge
27, rue Lambert (18th)
☎ 01 46 06 15 11
Closed Sat and Sun
[2]

Well-known wine bar, authentic atmosphere.

Au Virage Lepic
Ⓜ Abbesses
61, rue Lepic (18th)
☎ 01 42 52 46 79
[2]

Traditional cuisine in a pleasant atmosphere.

Beauvilliers
Ⓜ Lamarck-Caulaincourt
52, rue Lamarck (18th)
☎ 01 42 54 54 42
Closed Sun and Mon lunch
[3]

Impeccable service in this Montmartre restaurant.

La Coopérative
Ⓜ Guy Moquet
7, rue Lagille (18th)
☎ 01 42 29 26 65
Mon–Thurs 8am–8pm, Fri 8am–2am, Sat 4pm–2am
[1]

Cultural café; wholefood snacks from products favouring sustainable development, wi-fi connection and bookshelf.

Au Rendez-Vous de la Marine
Ⓜ Jaurès
14, quai de la Loire (19th)
☎ 01 42 49 33 40
[2]

A century-old soup kitchen on the Ourcq canal; plain but good food, trendy atmosphere.

FRENCH BREAD

Some clichés die hard. Very few Frenchmen still wear a beret, but you would have thought the *baguette* was untouchable. Wrong. By the 1970s, the quality of French bread was plunging in a downward spiral of mass production and changing eating habits—doctors, French doctors, were saying bread was not good for your health.

Along with packaged sliced bread, supermarkets began to stock, factory-produced, the once sacred baguette in an insipid, tasteless and, in an age of detergents, "whiter than white" form that, despite artificial preservatives, went stale almost before it got to the table. The little local baker went into a depression deep as the back-room freezer in which supermarkets stocked their baguettes.

Rising from the Ashes

Then, since the 1990s, the Frenchmen's nature as perennial *râleurs* (malcontents) has won the day. Backed by a new generation of doctors lauding good bread's nutritive qualities, customers want the bread that grandma remembers—baked in wood-ash to be crisp on the outside, tender, slightly moist on the inside, above all tasting of real unbleached wheat flour. Instead of copying the supermarket's mass produced excuses for bread, local bakers offer *baguettes à l'ancienne* ("in the old style") or baguette-tradition, a little dearer but lasting longer. They are rewarded with lines around the block. "Whiter than white" is going out of style in favour of untreated off-white and wholemeal breads. Other old-fashioned or new-fangled breads are popular, using a variety of cereals and powdered with cumin, poppy- or sesame seeds for bread-rolls (*petits pains*), big round *couronnes* or flat *fougasses* flavoured with olives or bacon-bits.

A Separate Case
Some French bakers remained impervious to this bread crisis, notably Poilâne (8, rue Cherche-Midi, 6th). Wood-baked after prolonged natural yeast-fermentation, its great round loaf called *une miche* has become world-famous (literally, since it can be sold fresh anywhere within 48 hours of baking). It is a café favourite for *croque-monsieur* (open-faced grilled cheese and ham sandwich). On the principle of "If you can't beat them, join them", Paris supermarkets now sell Poilâne bread, too—sliced.

Best Baguettes?
Among winners of the city's annual "best baguette" prize, try on the Left Bank: Kayser, 8 rue Monge, 5th; Right Bank: Julien, 75 rue Saint-Honoré, 1st.

DU PAIN OR NOT DU PAIN?
The *baguette* weighs, officially 250 g.
The *baguette-tradition* is a bit smaller, 150–200 g.
The double-size baguette, known just as *un pain*, weighs in at around 450 g.
The *bâtard* is a fatter, smaller version of the baguette, 150 g, but is now less common than the *demi-baguette* (half-baguette).
A *ficelle* ("string") is thinner and smaller, and may also be known as *une flûte*.
Increasingly popular, *un épi*, the same size as a baguette but nicely shaped like an ear of corn, has pointed edges easy to break off.

CityNights

The best way of finding out what's on is to invest €0.40 in the *Pariscope* or *l'Officiel des Spectacles,* weekly listings magazines with information on all the entertainment that livens up Parisian nights. *Pariscope* has an English supplement edited by *Time Out,* with reviews, a rundown of the club scene and information on events in English.

Tickets are usually put on sale two weeks before opening night. Book seats through your travel agent, your hotel concierge, at Virgin Megastore, 52, av. des Champs-Elysées, at the FNAC at Forum des Halles (level −3), or at the venues themselves. Half-price theatre tickets for performances the same day are sold at Kiosque Théâtre, Place de la Madeleine (Tues–Sat 12.30–8pm). A commission is charged. Special prices are available for children, students (with International Student Card) and senior citizens (over 60).

Theatres	114
Nightclubs	114
Jazz clubs and piano bars	115
Cabaret and café-théâtre	116
Concert halls and shows	117

L'Opéra Garnier

THEATRES

Comédie-Française-Richelieu
Ⓜ Palais-Royal
2, rue de Richelieu (1st)
☎ 08 25 10 16 80
Classic drama.

Opéra Comique-Salle Favart
Ⓜ Richelieu-Drouot
Pl. Boieldieu (2nd)
☎ 08 25 01 01 23
Opera and operettas.

Opéra Garnier
Ⓜ Opéra
Pl. de l'Opéra (2nd)
☎ 08 92 89 90 90
Classical and modern ballet in the superbly renovated Opéra.

Théâtre de la Ville
Ⓜ Châtelet
2, pl. du Châtelet (4th)
☎ 01 42 74 22 77

Comédie-Française du Vieux-Colombier
Ⓜ St-Sulpice
21, rue du Vieux-Colombier (6th)
☎ 01 44 39 87 00
The troupe of the Comédie Française performs classical and contemporary plays at this venue.

Odéon-Théâtre de l'Europe
Ⓜ Odéon
ⓇⒺⓇ Luxembourg
1, pl. de l'Odéon (6th)
☎ 01 44 85 40 40
Travelling European companies perform (in their own language) at the newly renovated Odéon theatre, and also in the Berthier workshops:
8, bd Berthier (17th)
Ⓜ Porte de Clichy

Théâtre des Champs-Elysées
Ⓜ Alma-Marceau
15, av. Montaigne (8th)
☎ 01 49 52 50 50

Théâtre Marigny-Robert Hossein
Ⓜ Champs-Elysées-Clémenceau
Carré Marigny (8th)
☎ 01 53 96 70 00
You can count on seeing at least one famous French actor in one of the two Marigny theatres.

Opéra-Bastille
Ⓜ Bastille
Pl. de la Bastille (11th)
☎ 08 92 89 90 90
Operas, operettas, symphony concerts and

L'Opéra Bastille

cabaret feature on the bill of the modern opera house.

Théâtre national de Chaillot
Ⓜ Trocadéro
Pl. du Trocadéro (16th)
☎ 01 53 65 30 00

Théâtre national de la Colline
Ⓜ Gambetta
15, rue Malte-Brun (20th)
☎ 01 44 62 52 52
Plays by young French authors are performed here, in two theatres.

NIGHTCLUBS

Some of the trendiest nightclubs require a membership card (but you can always try charming the doormen). Things warm up around midnight, and the action lasts till 5 or 6 am.

La Scala
Ⓜ Louvre
188bis, rue de Rivoli (1st)
☎ 01 42 61 64 00

All kinds of music and dance on three floors.

Rex Club
Ⓜ Bonne-Nouvelle
5, bd Poissonnières (2nd)
☎ 01 42 36 10 96
House, techno, top DJs, a varied programme and worldwide reputation.

Les Bains-Douches
Ⓜ Etienne-Marcel
7, rue du Bourg-l'Abbé (3rd)
☎ 01 53 01 40 60
Fashion models and starlets frequent this club in the former public baths. Japanese restaurant.

Le Queen
Ⓜ George V
102, av. des Champs-Elysées (8th)
☎ 01 53 89 08 90
Former gay club now open to all communities.

Le Bus Palladium
Ⓜ Blanche
6, rue Fontaine (9th)
☎ 01 53 21 07 33
Free admission and drinks for the girls on the Tuesday ladies' night.

La Casbah
Ⓜ Ledru-Rollin
18, rue Forge-Royale (11th)
☎ 01 43 71 04 39
The restaurant includes a club and bar with a décor inspired by the film *Casablanca*.

Batofar
Ⓜ Bibliothèque François Mitterrand
11, quai François-Mauriac (13th)
☎ 01 56 29 10 00
Two bars and a disco with electronic music on a boat on the Seine. Space for up to 300 people. Concerts are organized.

La Guinguette Pirate
Ⓜ Quai de la Gare
Quai François-Mauriac (13th)
below the BNF
☎ 01 53 61 08 49
Lively nightclub on a barge; dances, concerts.

La Locomotive
Ⓜ Blanche
90, bd de Clichy (18th)
☎ 01 53 41 88 88
Disco and theme nights, on the site of the former Bal du Moulin Rouge.

JAZZ CLUBS AND PIANO BARS

Le Baiser salé
Ⓜ Châtelet
58, rue des Lombards (1st)
☎ 01 42 33 37 71

Live jazz, young crowd, lots of swing.

Le Duc des Lombards
Ⓜ Châtelet
42, rue des Lombards (1st)
☎ 01 42 33 22 88
Big Parisian jazz scene with internationally renowned musicians in a romantic venue.

Le Petit Opportun
Ⓜ Châtelet
15, rue des Lavandières-Sainte-Opportune (1st)
☎ 01 42 36 01 36
Concerts from 11.30pm.

Harry's New York Bar
Ⓜ Opéra
5, rue Daunou (2nd)
☎ 01 42 61 71 14
Famous American bar. Go downstairs for the cosy piano bar. Large choice of cocktails here.

Caveau de la Huchette
Ⓜ St-Michel
5, rue de la Huchette (5th)
☎ 01 43 26 65 05
Every night from 9.30pm
Traditional jazz.

Le Petit Journal St-Michel
Ⓡ Luxembourg
71, bd Saint-Michel (5th)
☎ 01 43 26 28 59
Closed Sunday
Famous musicians and friendly atmosphere. Great reputation.

Le Bar du Lutétia
Ⓜ Sèvres-Babylone
Hôtel Lutétia (6th)
☎ 01 49 54 46 46
Live jazz from Wednesday to Saturday from 10.15pm.

The cabaret scene is alive and kicking.

Le Bilboquet
Ⓜ St-Germain-des-Prés
13, rue Saint-Benoît (6th)
☎ 01 45 48 81 84
One of the most famous jazz clubs in Paris, still going strong.

New Morning
Ⓜ Château d'Eau
7–9, rue des Petites-Ecuries (10th)
☎ 01 45 23 51 41
The world's most famous musicians play here.

Jazz Club Lionel Hampton
Ⓜ Porte Maillot
Hôtel le Méridien
81, bd Gouvion-Saint-Cyr (17th)
☎ 01 40 68 30 42
Top-class musicians play from 10.30pm–2am. Big choice of cocktails and pure malt whiskies.

CABARET AND CAFÉ-THÉÂTRE

Caveau de la République
Ⓜ République

1, bd Saint-Martin (3rd)
☎ 01 42 78 44 45
Stand-up comedians, political satire, in the great Parisian tradition.

Café de la Gare
Ⓜ Hôtel de Ville
41, rue du Temple (4th)
☎ 01 42 78 52 51
The former Inn of the Golden Eagle can be considered the cradle of modern French comedians. Some of the big screen names started out here way back in the 1970s, beginning the tradition of irreverent café-théâtre.

Paradis Latin
Ⓜ Cardinal-Lemoine
28, rue du Cardinal-Lemoine (5th)
☎ 01 43 25 28 28
Dinner, live orchestra and girly revue.

Le Don Camilo
Ⓜ St-Germain-des-Prés
10, rue des Saints-Pères (6th)
☎ 01 42 60 82 84
Dinner and show spiced up with comic sketches.

Crazy Horse Paris
Ⓜ George-V
12, av. George-V (8th)
☎ 01 47 23 32 32
Sun–Fri shows at 8.15 and 10.45pm, Sat at 7, 9.30 and 11.45pm
Said to be the best strip-tease in Paris, maybe in the world.

Lido
Ⓜ George-V
116bis, av. des Champs-Elysées (8th)
☎ 01 40 76 56 10
Shows every night at 9.30 and 11.30pm
One of the world's most famous cabarets, created in 1946 and producing the famous troupe of Bluebells dancing girls.

Folies Bergère
Ⓜ Cadet, Grands Boulevards
32, rue Richer (9th)
☎ 08 92 68 16 50
Closed Monday
The stuff of legend.

Pau Brazil
Ⓜ Charles de Gaulle-Etoile
32, rue de Tilsitt (17th)
☎ 01 53 57 77 66
Brazilian atmosphere, dinner and show in the old Etoile swimming pool.

Bal du Moulin Rouge
Ⓜ Blanche
82, bd de Clichy (18th)
☎ 01 53 09 82 82
Birthplace of the cancan. Dinner dance at 7pm, shows at 9 and 11pm.

Chez Michou
Ⓜ Pigalle
80, rue des Martyrs (18th)
☎ 01 46 06 16 04
Hilarious drag-show hosted by Michou, always dressed in blue, who created this cabaret in 1956. Show at 11pm. Dinner 8.30pm (reservation compulsory).

CONCERT HALLS AND SHOWS

Olympia Bruno Coquatrix
Ⓜ Opéra, Madeleine
28, bd des Capucines (9th)
☎ 08 92 68 33 68

Palais Omnisports de Paris Bercy
Ⓜ Bercy
8, bd de Bercy (12th)
☎ 01 40 02 60 60

Parc des Princes
Ⓜ Porte de Saint-Cloud, Porte d'Auteuil
24, rue du Commandant Guibauld (16th)
☎ 01 47 43 72 56 or 3275

Le Zénith de Paris
Ⓜ Porte de Pantin
211, av. Jean-Jaurès (19th)
☎ 01 42 08 60 00

Stade de France
Ⓜ Stade de France
Saint-Denis-Porte de Paris
☎ 08 92 70 09 00

cityFacts

Babysitting	120
Climate	120
Customs and Entry Formalities	120
Disabled	120
Driving	121
Electricity	121
Emergencies	121
Hours	122
Lost and Found	122
Money	122
Public Holidays	123
Safety Precautions	123
Telephone	123
Time	124
Tipping	124
Toilets	124
Tourist Information Office	124
Tours	125
Transport	126
Velib' and Bicycle Hire	129

Babysitting

Ask at your hotel or contact:
BabyChou Service: ☎01 43 13 33 23, www.babychou.com
Baby Sitting Services: ☎01 46 21 33 16, www.babysittingservices.com

Climate

Paris enjoys a mild continental climate, with daily temperatures of 15–30°C (59–86°F) or more in summer and 3–10°C (37–50°F) in winter. It's advisable to take a folding umbrella as Paris gets a surprising amount of rain. July and August are often stiflingly hot.

Customs and Entry Formalities

In principle, travel between France and other parties to the 1995 Schengen agreement (Belgium, Germany, Luxembourg, Netherlands, Portugal, Spain) is without documentation check at immigration controls. However, passports are still required for those entering from Britain.

Passengers over 17 years of age arriving from non-EU countries may import, tax-free: 200 cigarettes, 50 cigars or 250 g tobacco, 1 litre spirits and 2 litres wine. For passengers from EU countries the quantities are much higher, but on duty-paid goods, for personal use.

Articles purchased in France are subject to VAT, or value-added tax. If you have spent at least €175 in any one shop, reside outside the EU, and are leaving France for a non-EU country, you may reclaim this tax (13% return after administration fees). Ask the shopkeeper for the *détaxe* papers.

Disabled

The major museums will provide a wheelchair if you ring in advance with your request. Many have an escort service as well. At the Louvre, there's a special lift for the disabled under the glass pyramid to the reception hall, where you pick up your wheelchair. In older galleries, guards will even open up doors closed to the general public to provide easier wheelchair access. The Louvre will suggest special tours planned for good mobility.

The Tourist Office publishes a brochure entitled *Paris est à vous,* in which the places are coded with symbols indicating wheelchair access and facilities for various handicaps. You will find more information on the tourist office website: www.parisinfo.com. Métro line 14 and RER line A are partly wheelchair-accessible. The association Les Compagnons du Voyage, created by the RATP and SNCF, has a service by which the disabled are accompanied during their journey. ☎01 58 76 08 33.

The English-language book *Access in Paris* is available from W. H. Smith, 248, rue de Rivoli or can be downloaded from www.accessinparis.org.

Driving
The **speed limit** is 50 kph (30 mph) in town, 80 kph (50 mph) on ring roads, and 130 kph (80 mph) on motorways. France drives on the right. Seat belts must be worn in both front and back seats. Children under 10 may not sit in the front seat. Horns should not be sounded in town. Do not drive in bus lanes. You must have a safety jacket that can be accessed without leaving the vehicle.

Parking places have card-operated meters, with hourly tariffs ranging between €1 and €2 per hour and a maximum stay of 2 hours (cards can be bought in *bureaux de tabac*). Spaces in covered car parks cost about €2 per hour. Badly parked cars may be towed away to the *fourrière*, where they will be returned after payment of a fine of around €150.

For driving information, call Centre Régional d'Informations Routières, ☎08 26 02 20 22.

Electricity
The current is 220-volt, 50 cycles AC. Plugs have two round prongs.

Emergencies
Police: dial **17**; fire brigade *(pompiers)*: **18**; SAMU (ambulance): **15**
European emergency phone number: **112**
SOS Médecins, for 24-hour house calls: ☎01 47 07 77 77
SOS Dentaire, dental emergencies: ☎01 43 37 51 00
For the **duty chemist**, phone the police on **17**
Pharmacie Les Champs: 84, av. des Champs-Elysées (8th), Ⓜ George V ☎01 45 62 02 41, open 24 hours a day.
American Hospital: 63, bd Victor Hugo, 92202 Neuilly, Ⓜ Porte Maillot and bus 82, ☎01 46 41 25 25.

Franco-British Hospital: 3, rue Barbès, 92300 Levallois-Perret, Ⓜ Anatole France, ☏ 01 46 39 22 22.

British nationals are entitled to use the medical services of the French social security system but need a European Health Card. Non-EU citizens are advised to take out health insurance before their trip.

Hours

Banks open Monday to Friday or Tuesday to Saturday 9am–5pm. Bureaux de change usually keep later hours and open Saturday and Sunday as well. Chequepoint operates a 24-hour change at 150, av. des Champs-Elysées.
Post offices open Monday to Friday 8am–7pm, Saturday 8am–noon. The Central Post Office, 52, rue du Louvre (1st), is open 24 hours a day, 7 days a week. ☏ 01 40 28 76 00
Food shops generally open Tuesday to Saturday 9am–1pm and 4–7pm. Some open on Monday afternoon or Sunday morning.
Boutiques open fairly late in the morning, 10.30, 11am or even noon, to 6.30 or 7pm, sometimes later.
The **department stores** all have one late closing *(nocturne)* per week.

Lost and Found

If you discover you have lost or been robbed, head to the nearest police station and make a declaration. You will be given a receipt, which you must retain for possible insurance claims. For objects lost in the métro or bus, inquire immediately at the terminus. If the object hasn't been handed in, inquire at the lost and found office (you must visit in person or write, indicating the date, place and time of loss and a description of the object): **Bureau des objets trouvés**, 36, rue des Morillons (15th), Ⓜ Convention ☏ 08 21 00 25 25. Mon–Thurs 8.30am–5pm, Friday 8.30am–4.30pm.

Money

The Euro, divided into 100 *centimes*. Large notes, of 200 and 500 euros, are sometimes refused. Credit cards are usually accepted, but there may be a minimum limit, and smaller restaurants and hotels frequently insist on cash. If you want to use your card to withdraw money from ATMs, check with your bank that it is valid abroad. There is usually a commission charge for each withdrawal. Travellers cheques are widely accepted. You need your passport to cash them.

Public holidays
Banks and post offices are closed on the following *fêtes nationales*:

January 1	New Year's Day
May 1	Labour Day
May 8	Victory Day, 1945
July 14	Bastille Day
August 15	Assumption
November 1	All Saints' Day
November 11	Armistice Day, 1918
December 25	Christmas Day
Movable:	Easter Monday, Ascension Day, Whit Monday

When a public holiday falls on a Tuesday or Thursday, people often take the intervening Monday or Friday off to make a long weekend.

Safety Precautions
Keep valuable objects, large amounts of money, your passport and travel tickets in the hotel safe and to carry only a little cash and a credit card. Travelling on the métro or on a bus late at night isn't advisable. Beware of pickpockets in the métro. Never carry your money in a rucksack. When you park your car, remove the radio-cassette-CD player and any valuables.

Telephone
You can place local or international calls from any public phone booth, of which there are two kinds: those that require coins, still found in cafés, and those that function with a phone card, or *télécarte*. The cards are on sale in post offices, principal métro and RER stations, SNCF (train) ticket counters, France Télécom agencies, and tobacconists. Calls are cheaper after 7.30pm and on weekends. You can also buy a pre-paid card (€15) which may be more economical for calling abroad.

All French telephone numbers, with the exception of services, consist of 10 digits. To call anywhere in Paris or the rest of France, you have to dial the full 10-digit number. Numbers starting with 08 generally cost €0.30/min.

To make an international call from Paris, dial 00, the country code (1 for USA and Canada, 44 for UK) then the area code (without the initial 0), and the local number.

Directory enquiries: dial 118 and the three figures corresponding to the phone company you want to use, e.g. 118 007 (Bottin), 118 712 (France Telecom), 118 218 (Le Numero).

Time
France follows GMT + 1. Hence 5pm in Paris is 4pm in London and 11am in New York. Daylight saving time (GMT + 2) runs from late March to end September. French time is based on the 24-hour system; that is, midnight to noon is written as 0.00 to 12.00, and noon to midnight as 12.00 to 24.00. So 14 h 30 means 2.30pm.

Tipping
Restaurants and cafés automatically include service charges in the bill. Taxi drivers should receive 10 per cent of the fare, a lavatory attendant expects a small tip (usually there's a conspicuous saucer), and a hotel porter should be tipped at least €1 per bag.

Toilets
Scattered throughout the city are the coin-operated self-cleaning cubicles called Sanisettes. Failing these, use the facilities of a café—but order at least a coffee (you may have to ask for the key at the counter). Otherwise use those in department stores, or nip into one of the big hotels. Toilets may be marked *Femmes* or *Dames* for women; *Hommes* or *Messieurs* for men; or simply *Toilettes* or WC.

Tourist Information Offices
☎ 08 92 68 30 00 (0,34€/min) www.parisinfo.com
Pyramides (Central Office) (1st): 25, rue des Pyramides. June–Oct daily 9am–7pm; Nov–May Mon–Sat 10am–7pm, Sun and holidays 11am–7pm; closed May 1.
Carrousel du Louvre (1st): Place de la Pyramide inversée. Daily 10am–6pm.

Gare de l'Est (10th): Place du 11 novembre 1918; arrivals TGV Grandes Lignes, exit Cour d'Alsace. Mon–Sat 7am–8pm.
Gare du Nord (10th): New Ile de France station, under the glass dome, daily 8am–6pm, closed Jan 1, May 1 and December 25.
Gare de Lyon (12th): Arrivals Hall Grandes Lignes, Mon–Sat 8am–6pm; closed May 1.

Tours
Boat tours. Several companies offer cruises with commentary along the Seine and canals, or lunch, tea and dinner cruises:
Bateaux-Mouches: Pont de l'Alma, right bank, ☎ 01 42 25 96 10
Bateaux Parisiens Notre-Dame: Quai de Montebello, left bank (near Notre-Dame), ☎ 01 43 26 92 55
Bateaux Parisiens: Port de la Bourdonnais, left bank, ☎ 08 25 01 01 01 www.bateauxparisiens.com
Vedettes de Paris et de l'Ile-de-France: Port de Suffren, ☎ 01 47 05 71 29
Vedettes du Pont-Neuf: Square du Vert-Galant, ☎ 01 46 33 98 38
Canauxrama: 50, bd de la Bastille (11th) and 13, quai de la Loire (19th), ☎ 01 42 39 15 00
Paris Canal: from Musée d'Orsay (quai Anatole France) to Parc de la Villette and vice versa ☎ 01 42 40 96 97
Marina de Bercy: Port de Bercy, right bank, ☎ 01 43 43 40 30

Bus tours. The *Balabus* circulates around the main tourist sites every Sunday and public holiday from spring through summer, from 1.30 to 8.30pm from Gare de Lyon and frm 12.30–8pm from the Grande Arche de la Défense. A complete circuit takes 50 min. You can board at any stop showing the "Balabus" sign: Saint-Michel, Musée d'Orsay, Louvre, Concorde, Champs-Elysées, etc.

The *Montmartrobus* makes a tour of the Montmartre hill. Terminus at Place Pigalle and town hall *(mairie)* of the 18th arrondissement.

Private sightseeing companies like *Paris-Vision* or *Cityrama* run 2-hour tours with commentaries in many languages.

With *Cars Rouges*, ☎ 01 53 95 39 53, you can hop on and off as you like. Tickets are sold on the bus and valid two consecutive days.

Walking tours. For 2-hour guided tours in English, call Paris Walks, 01 48 09 21 40, www.paris-walks.com. Another company, Context, organizes walking seminars for groups of 6 on various themes (architecture, chocolate, boulevards, markets, bohemians, etc.) led by scholars and experts. For information see www.contextparis.com. If you want to join a guided tour in French, look under the heading *Conférences* in *Pariscope, l'Officiel des Spectacles* or the daily newspaper listings.

The "Planted Promenade" walkway runs 4.5 km (3 miles) east to west (about a third of it elevated above the traffic), along avenue Daumesnil, starting behind the Opéra Bastille and ending at the Bois de Vincennes. It is dotted with five gardens, and there are lanes for pedestrians and cyclists. Other itineraries available at the tourist office.

From the Austerlitz bridge to the Invalides bridge, a 5-km (3-mile) path along the quays is reserved for pedestrians. The particularly scenic stretch of embankment between the Sully and Iéna bridges has been designated by UNESCO as a World Heritage site.

Roller-blading. Every Friday night at 9.30pm, thousands of people gather in front of the Gare Montparnasse for a 3-hour tour of the boulevards, escorted by police on skates. Information on www.pari-roller.com

Transport

Métro. The underground is by far the handiest and quickest way of getting around. Locate your destination on the map and follow the lines by their colour, number and, to ensure that you find the right platform *(quai)*, the name of the terminus corresponding to the direction you're headed. This terminus is signposted on the platform and in all the access corridors. The itinerary of the line is displayed in the interior of the métro car. To transfer to another line, look for the orange *"Correspondance"* sign and follow the corridors to your new direction. If you are loaded with luggage, avoid changing lines or buying tickets at Châtelet-Les Halles, which is huge, chaotic and confusingly signposted.

Near the station exit *(Sortie)*, consult the map of the immediate neighbourhood and you'll find the way to your final destination. Exits are usually indicated for even *(pairs)* and odd *(impairs)* street numbers.

First departures from the terminus stations are at 5.30am; last arrivals at 1.15am Mon–Thurs and Sun, 2.15am on Fridays and Saturdays.

RER. This ultra-rapid transport system links Paris with the suburbs. You can switch easily from the métro to the RER, as the two networks are interconnected. Be sure to keep your ticket handy; you will need it when you leave the system and for spot-checks. An RER ticket from the suburbs to Paris is also valid on the métro.

The first trains leave the terminus stations at 5.30am; last arrivals at the terminus around 1.15am.

Bus. Explanatory information is posted at the bus stops. Stop a bus by raising your hand; inside, ring the buzzer to get off. The *Noctilien*, or night bus, travels 42 routes, every night between 0.30 and 5.30am.

Tram. A modern tram runs along the boulevards des Maréchaux, between the Pont du Garigliano and the Porte d'Ivry in the southern part of the 13th, 14th and 15th arrondissements.

Tickets for métro, bus and tram ("ticket t") are on sale singly (€1.60) or in booklets (*carnet*) of 10 (€11.40). One ticket is valid for 1.5hrs for a journey by métro or RER within Paris on any number of lines; one ticket is required for the bus as long as you stay on the same line. It's worth buying a pass:

Mobilis. Valid for one day on the bus network, métro and RER (except airport services), for 1 to 6 zones. Orly and Versailles are in zone 4, Roissy and Chessy (Disneyland Paris) in zone 5. Prices from €5.80 to €16.40.

Paris-Visite Card. Valid for 1, 2, 3 or 5 days over the entire network of the RATP, RER, SNCF Paris and Ile-de-Paris, Montmartrobus, Noctilien, and airport services, with an option of 3 or 6 zones. For 4 days it's slightly cheaper to buy 3+1 rather than 2+2. Prices from €8.80 to €48.40. Half price for children from 4 to 11 years. The pass also offers discounts at several tourist sites.

For access to the métro or RER platforms, slide your pass into the turnstile slot. You need to do the same thing at the exit. In the bus, show your card to the conductor without punching it in the validating machine.

Batobus. Regularly scheduled boats make 8 stops along the Seine, from the Eiffel Tower to the Jardin des Plantes. Closed January. ☎ 08 25 05 01 01.

To and from Roissy Charles-de-Gaulle airport. CDGVal is a free shuttle link between the different terminals and the two railway stations Aéroport Charles de Gaulle 1 and Aéroport Charles de Gaulle 2 TGV, where you can get the RER (line B). It takes 35 minutes to reach central Paris. Departures every 10 to 15 min.

Roissybus leaves every 15 minutes for Paris Opéra.

Air France coaches Line 2 depart every 30 minutes and take 45 minutes to reach the centre of Paris. Drop-offs near Arc de Triomphe or Porte Maillot, alongside the Palais des Congrès.

To and from Orly airport. "Paris par le train" is a shuttle from the airport to the Pont de Rungis station where you can get the RER (line C). It takes 35 minutes to the centre of Paris.

Orlybus departs every 15–20 minutes for Place Denfert-Rochereau.

Air France Line 1 buses run every 30 minutes and take 30 minutes to reach the city centre. Drop-off points are Invalides or the Hôtel Méridien Montparnasse.

Orlyval automatic métro runs every 4 to 7 minutes during the day and takes 8 minutes to the RER station of Antony. From there the RER takes about 20 minutes to the centre of Paris.

Jetbus is a rapid link between the airport and Villejuif/Louis Aragon métro station, on line 7.

To and from Beauvais airport. Bus shuttles link the airport with the Palais des Congrès, Porte Maillot, taking about 60 min. Information www.aeroportbeauvais.com ☎ 32 46 or from abroad: +33 8 92 68 20 66.

General information. For up-to-date information on Paris transport, strikes, prices, etc: ☎ 08 92 68 77 14 or www.ratp.fr/.

Taxis. ☎ 01 45 30 30 30. The running charge is displayed on a meter. It consists of an initial fixed fee (€2.20), plus the price of the journey, with a tariff varying according to the time of day. The minimum charge is €6. One piece of luggage is carried free, but every other bag weighing more than 5 kg and placed in the boot entails an extra charge of €1 (not shown on the meter). Taxis are not obliged to carry more than three passengers. The driver may be persuaded to consent to a fourth (adult), but he will charge a supplement of €2.95. A taxi from one of the airports to the centre of Paris can cost up to €60 or more. Complaints are handled by the **Service des Taxis**, Préfecture de Police, 36, rue des Morillons, 75015 Paris. Give the number of the taxi and the date, time and reason for your complaint.

SNCF Trains. For information or reservations, call 3635; from abroad call ☎ +33 8 92 35 35 35. www.sncf.fr.

Velib' and Bicycle Hire

Velib' is a system of bicycle hire set up by the Mairie de Paris. More than 20,000 bicycles are available at 1450 self-service pick-up points located near métro stations and bus stops. An annual pass costs €29 (to be ordered on-line, cheque deposit of €150 required); short-term 1-day, €1, and 7-day, €5 passes are available directly at the pick-up points, using a credit card. In both cases a deposit of €150 is required. The first half-hour is free; the next half hour €1, second half-hour €2, then €4 for each extra half hour (deducted from your account). For more details see www.velib.paris.fr
Otherwise, you can hire a bike at:
Paris Bike Tour: 38, rue de Saintonge (3rd) Ⓜ Filles du Calvaire, République ☎01 42 74 22 14 Daily 9.30am–6.30pm (reservation recommended)
Paris à Vélo c'est sympa!: 22, rue Alphonse Baudin (11th) Ⓜ St-Sébastien-Froissart, Richard-Lenoir ☎01 48 87 60 01. Closed Tues. 9.30am–1pm, 2–5.30pm (Sat, Sun to 6pm). Also guided tours (upon reservation) in French and English.

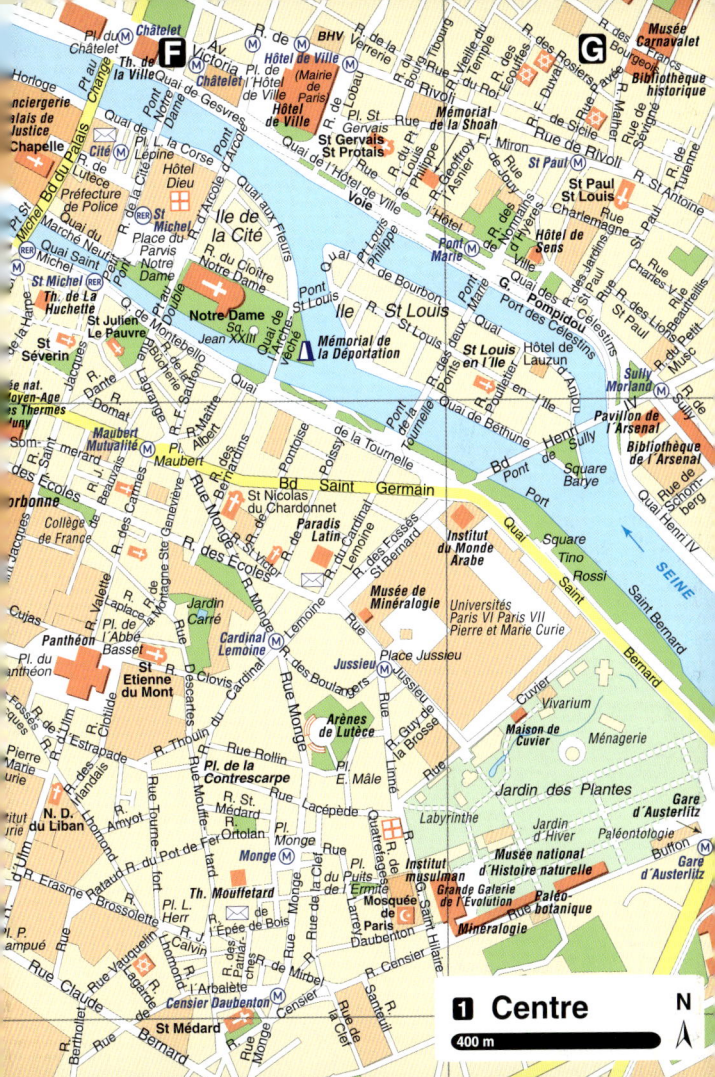

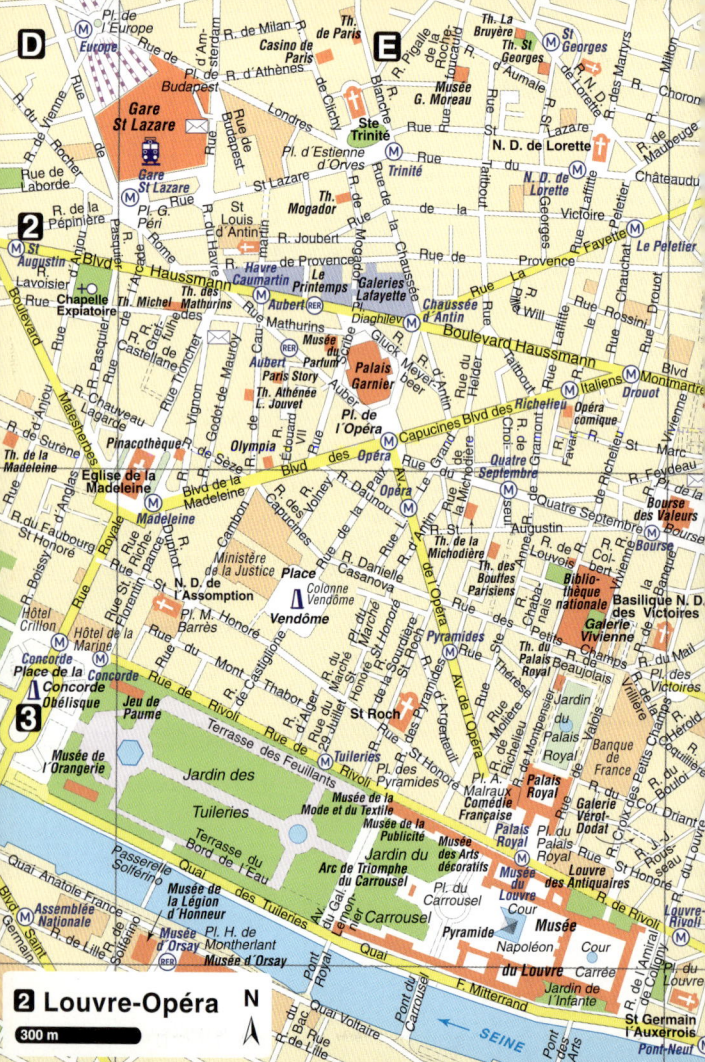